"President Scott W. Sunquist has given us a gripping book on world Christianity! Its new historiography unlocks the results of Christian preaching, thought, and practice in diverse contexts. Its rich biographical and pedagogical narratives along with their rational and passionate presentation are both informative and transformative. It recognizes the valuable contributions of indigenous Christians with their own resources to their local congregations; their lively and active Christianity manifests itself as 'cruciform apostolicity' because it addresses the local, ever-changing sentiments and it also opposes the systemic evil among them. This book frees and enriches the knowledge horizon of readers, whose mindset has thus far been conditioned by Euro-American norms, assumptions, and approaches. With transformed insights they learn to discover the kaleidoscopic shapes and expressions of Christian life, their collective thought, and witnesses. Thus this book invites them to enjoy a fresh 'historical journey into the fascinating and illuminating world of Christian history.'"

Daniel Jeyaraj, professor of world Christianity and the director of the Andrew Walls Centre for the Study of African and Asian Christianity at Liverpool Hope University, England

"In this elegantly crafted book, Sunquist distills decades of research in the historical materials of global Christianity in order to convey the theological meaning they hold. In them, he finds the concepts of time (creation and incarnation), cross (suffering and mission), and glory (humility and hope). They inform how we tell and, more importantly, live the story. Rich with quotable lines and pastoral insights, Sunquist gives us a superior book that will serve as a resource for people of faith everywhere."

Grant Wacker, Gilbert T. Rowe Distinguished Professor of Christian History at Duke Divinity School

"Scott Sunquist introduces a comprehensive view of the history of Christianity and a meditative theological approach to mission. For Sunquist, the history of Christianity is the reading and writing of the action of the Divine in the world and among people. The story of Christianity gives hope to humanity and tells the story of the past with the future in view. Sunquist's writing is informed by deep experience and observation of the histories of people. This book is a valuable guide to re-center the writing of Christian history."

Lois Farag, professor of history of early Christianity at Luther Seminary

"Much contemporary writing implies that there is no such thing as Christianity, only a bewildering multiplicity of local appropriations of what was once the religion of the Western world. Scott Sunquist's book provides a telling riposte. Both profoundly theological and historically well-informed, it powerfully argues the case that the Jesus movement today is held together by the same convictions as it was at the beginning —that history begins with divine creation, turns on divine intervention in the person of Jesus Christ, and ends with the glory of the completed kingdom of God."

Brian Stanley, professor of world Christianity at the University of Edinburgh

"*The Shape of Christian History* should be every Christian's companion when learning or teaching about the history of our rapidly growing global church in all its breadth and complexity. Scott Sunquist's extended essay on Christian historiography helps us to remember that meaningful history is the 'retelling of a story of the past with purpose and passion.' He assists us in our careful and thoughtful reading and writing about God's transformative work through the body of Christ over time—especially in light of the dramatic changes in Christian demographics over the past few decades. Such a valuable guidebook can only emanate from a lifetime of research and scholarship, and such is absolutely the case with Sunquist's important and engaging work."

Douglas M. Strong, Paul T. Walls Professor of Wesleyan Studies and the History of Christianity at Seattle Pacific University

"Precious things come in small boxes, so this gem of a book, despite its petite size, packs in more than three decades of research and writing on the history of Christianity. It proposes a way of reading church history that is properly theological, in which the articles of faith regarding creation, incarnation, the cross, and resurrection function as beacons illuminating the meaning of history. Only a scholar of Sunquist's learning and wisdom can produce this tour de force. It must be required reading for all students of theology and church history."

Peter C. Phan, Ignacio Ellacuria Chair of Catholic Social Thought at Georgetown University

"The need for fresh approaches to the historical study of Christianity as a global faith (with growing heartlands outside the West) is widely acknowledged. Yet how to make sense of Christianity as a movement in history with multitudinous expressions around the world and simultaneously composing a single universal community of faith remains a complex issue. In this important study, Scott Sunquist, a leading historian of world Christianity, makes the case for an interpretive framework that views Christianity as an historic movement with a transformative message centered on the person of Jesus Christ. This approach queries the 'Christianities' construct, which inherently legitimizes a Western substructure, and assails the notion of neutrality in historical writing. Sunquist adopts a historical lens that is unabashedly missional and theological (the cross gets significant attention). His treatment weaves historical analysis, biographical accounts, personal experience, and scholarly critique in a manner that offers important insights into the study of Christian history in a new era."

Jehu J. Hanciles, D. W. and Ruth Brooks Professor of World Christianity and director of the World Christianity Program at Candler School of Theology, Emory University

Scott W. Sunquist

President of Gordon-Conwell
Theological Seminary

**Continuity
and Diversity
in the Global
Church**

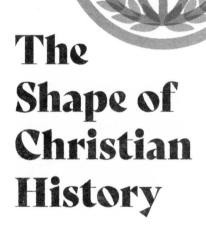

The
Shape of
Christian
History

ivp
Academic
An imprint of InterVarsity Press
Downers Grove, Illinois

InterVarsity Press
P.O. Box 1400 | Downers Grove, IL 60515-1426
ivpress.com | email@ivpress.com

InterVarsity Press® is the publishing division of InterVarsity Christian Fellowship/USA®. For more information,
visit intervarsity.org.

Scripture quotations, unless otherwise noted, are from the New Revised Standard Version Bible,
copyright © 1989 National Council of the Churches of Christ in the United States of America. Used by permission.
All rights reserved worldwide.

The publisher cannot verify the accuracy or functionality of website URLs used in this book beyond the date
of publication.

Cover design and image composite: David Fassett
Interior design: Daniel van Loon

ISBN 978-1-5140-0222-3 (print) | ISBN 978-1-5140-0223-0 (digital)

Printed in the United States of America ∞

Library of Congress Cataloging-in-Publication Data
Names: Sunquist, Scott W. (Scott William), 1953- author.
Title: The shape of Christian history : continuity and diversity in the
  global church / Scott W. Sunquist.
Description: Downers Grove, IL : IVP Academic, [2022] | Includes
  bibliographical references and index.
Identifiers: LCCN 2022004480 (print) | LCCN 2022004481 (ebook) | ISBN
  9781514002223 (print) | ISBN 9781514002230 (digital)
Subjects: LCSH: Church history–Historiography.
Classification: LCC BR138 .S88 2022 (print) | LCC BR138 (ebook) | DDC
  270.1072–dc23/eng/20220223
LC record available at https://lccn.loc.gov/2022004480
LC ebook record available at https://lccn.loc.gov/2022004481

26   25   24   23   22 | 6   5   4   3   2   1

To my father,

Virgil W. Sunquist (1925–2013),

and my mother,

Christine J. Sunquist (1924–2003),

who taught me the precious values of family, church, and tradition.

Ut in omnibus glorificatur Deus

Contents

Preface

THE FOLLOWING VOLUME owes its existence to two requests. Understanding these requests will help to explain the nature of this volume. First, I was asked to do the Princeton Students' Lectures on Missions in October 2009. This request gave me the opportunity to put together a number of thoughts about Christianity in history that had been bouncing around in my lectures, courses, and articles for the previous ten or fifteen years.

I have been a student of history since my university days, when I found myself attracted to every possible history course available. Like my taste in music, my taste in history has always been eclectic. I took courses in the history of classical opera, the history of work and leisure, the history and geography of economic activity, as well as the history of Russia (taught through novels). Thus, I knew my lectures would be historical, dealing with newer themes that had come to my attention though years of reading about history in Asia, Latin America, and Africa. Princeton Theological Seminary had a similarly expansive experience in mission and in sending out its students in mission and preparing national leaders from all corners of the world. Princeton also shared with me the love of ecumenics, "the science of the Church universal," as John Mackay refers to it.[1] It was a good match.

---

[1]John Mackay, *The Science of the Church Universal* (Englewood Cliffs, NJ: Prentice-Hall, 1964).

The Students' Lectures on Missions are the oldest series of lectures at Princeton Theological Seminary, and a look at a sampling of the past lecturers gives a history of mission thinking for the past century. I hope some future PhD student will do a dissertation on the development of missiology as seen through these lectures.

The list of lectures is a fascinating and impressive selection of global mission scholars that covers the last 130 years. As early as 1905 the voices of non-Western scholars were being heard, and throughout the years some of the great ecumenical voices—and many non-Presbyterians—were heard as well. Thus, I would like to thank the Princeton Seminary faculty, former president Iain Torrance, and former dean Darrell Guder for the opportunity to stand in such a line of missional scholarship. I also thank them for giving me this opportunity to pull together threads of questions, hunches, and ideas that have been showing up in my research and writing the past thirty-five years since I first arrived at Princeton to do my graduate work.

The second request, which was actually the first request chronologically, was to work with Dale Irvin to write what became the *History of the World Christian Movement*.[2] That particular project gathered a community of scholars together to write Christian history as a global movement rather than as a Western religion with foreign embassies. The process of writing with forty or fifty scholars looking over one's shoulder (at times breathing down one's neck) is a terrible and wonderful thing. On one hand it is like a fifteen-year dissertation defense, much as I imagine purgatory to be like if I believed in it. But on the other hand, it is also a little bit like heaven, with the great diversity of Christians together representing their traditions and speaking their minds and hearts. What this project meant is that fifty or so scholars from around the world had the precious opportunity to hear, read, and discuss Christianity from multiple perspectives.

---

[2]Scott Sunquist and Dale Irvin, *History of the World Christian Movement*, 2 vols. (Maryknoll, NY: Orbis, 2001–2012).

None of us will ever turn back from that commitment. For me, as a historian, it was a great awakening.

The result of that long-term labor of researching, outlining, and writing the history of the *world* Christian movement is that we developed a new historiography that changed the way we understand Christianity as an amazing Christian *movement*. Common assumptions about how Christianity develops and about how theology and liturgy develop had to be modified and at times completely rethought. The remarkable story of twentieth-century Christianity was the stimulus to completely rethink, in a global community, how to understand and write Christian history.[3] This volume is an introduction into this new way of understanding Christian history. It is also a guide to how we should read and even critique Christian history and the church today.

Every scholar knows that she or he stands on the shoulders of those who have gone before and works in a community of colleagues asking similar questions and working with much of the same material. Thus, I must acknowledge some of my indebtedness to those who have gone before and to those who walk beside me. I have been fortunate to have been guided by and worked with both Sam and Eileen Moffett since 1984. Both are model scholars and passionate missionaries who have great love for the church, joy in Christian service, and love for Koreans. Other mentors, mostly from afar, have been Andrew Walls and David Bosch. When I was a doctoral student, I served on a search committee and tried to get both of them to come teach at Princeton Theological Seminary. Through the years they both have had a great influence on me and good relations with Princeton. For more than two decades Dale T. Irvin and I have worked together on the *History of the World Christian Movement* project. I have learned a great deal from him and

---

[3]For a perspective on this century, see Scott W. Sunquist, *The Unexpected Christian Century: The Reversal and Transformation of Global Christianity, 1900–2000* (Grand Rapids, MI: Baker Academic, 2015).

his expansive view of the church and love for the city. Dale and I were fortunate enough to have been guided in our writing of the *History of the World Christian Movement* volumes by former editor of Orbis Books, Bill Burrows. Rarely does one find such a gracious, strong-headed, winsome, intuitive, and supportive editor. Bill the theologian and missiologist has also become a fine historian and good friend through the years. One of the historians who was most helpful for me in working on volumes two and three of *History of the World Christian Movement* was Ogbu Kalu. Kalu was always strong in defending his positions, clear and exacting in bibliographic references, and at the end of the day a joyous and supportive colleague.

Finally, my thinking about how to understand Christian history as a movement has been greatly influenced by students and scholars in Asia. My first trip to Asia was in 1987. Speaking as a historian, that was not that long ago. Yet when I consider the work that many of my former students are doing and the creative forms of ministry and cultural adaptation that have developed, I am both amazed and provoked. They are part of the ongoing historical movement in Asia that I first studied in the 1980s when I took my first course on early Asian Christianity with Sam Moffett. Not only their ministry and missionary work but also Asian Christian historians have been my teachers. In recent history some very good scholarship has been coming from Asian scholars talking about their own history. These historians and practitioners have given a perspective on Christianity never before possible.

I wish to express my appreciation to the former Princeton Theological Seminary librarian and editor of *The Princeton Seminary Bulletin*, Stephen Crocco, for his collegial support and permission to use much of the material in chapter one that was first published in the *Bulletin*.[4] I also must acknowledge the generous gift of "tropical space"

---

[4]Scott Sunquist, "Time, the Lectures and Redemption," *Princeton Seminary Bulletin* 30 (2009): 180-92.

(or sacred space) that was given to Nancy and me by Jack and Judy Isherwood. Solitude, God's creation, and tropical heat helped me to do most of the writing on the draft of this volume. Dr. Thu En Yu and the faculty of Sabah Theological Seminary gave me more tropical space to write, and we are very grateful for the hospitality given us by both faculty and students. *Terimah kasih.*

I had hoped to finish this a decade ago, but in the meantime I have taken on administrative work and other writing projects that threatened the completion of this volume. I am thankful for my editor, Jon Boyd, for prodding me.

Once again I am grateful for a supportive (and growing) family. When I started this project, we had four children and two grandchildren. Now we have twelve grandchildren; I am just a slow writer and thinker. Once again, I especially am thankful for an encouraging and wise wife, Nancy. She helps me say no to other distractions in a way that always says yes to our call in Christian ministry. Thank you.

Introduction

THIS IS A BOOK ON HOW to both write and read Christian history, or what we often call "church history." This is also a volume about how to understand Christianity and the life we, as Christians, have in God.[1]

In January 2010 Professor Andrew Walls was giving a lecture in Aarhaus, Denmark, and in typical fashion quietly dropped a bombshell: "Western theology is too small for global Christianity today." Shaken, disturbed, and probably offended by the remark, Stanley Hauerwas asked what in the world he meant. Hauerwas is a good Western theologian and ethicist who could easily feel implicated in such a remark. I don't know that I heard the answer, but Walls's comment rings true for Christian historians who have been paying attention to the Majority World and know exactly what Walls was talking about. Others, for whom Christianity is still understood as a Western religion with normative Western forms of thought are, like Hauerwas, confused.[2]

No one ever dreamed that we would have the variety of forms of Christianity with such vigor outside the West that are only

---

[1]See Donald Fairbairn, *Life in the Trinity: An Introduction to Theology with the Help of the Church Fathers* (Downers Grove, IL: IVP Academic, 2009).

[2]Another expression of this gap, divide, or "hermeneutical schizophrenia" (as she calls it) is found in Esther E. Acolatse's *Powers, Principalities, and the Spirit: Biblical Realism in Africa and the West* (Grand Rapids, MI: Eerdmans, 2018).

tangentially related to Western theological forms and ideas. Christianity's remarkable transformation in the past two generations has been much faster than traditional seminaries and denominations could imagine. Global Christianity, the largest religion in the world, has proven much more nimble, dynamic, diverse, and vital than most of its institutions. This means that we must rethink basic assumptions about its core and its boundaries. But our seminary curricula and institutions are making minor adjustments when we really don't have a clue as to what major changes have taken place around us. We have become accustomed to this tame, caterpillar-like Christendom in the West, and suddenly it has become a butterfly and gone off where it will.

The reason for this book is related to the statement of Andrew Walls above. Our theological and historical categories and approaches that seemed to have served us well in the past are preventing us from embracing and appreciating the fullness of the Christian movement and its thought and life today. The student of Christianity in the twenty-first century has a unique opportunity to study and understand Christianity in all of its beautiful and culturally transformative diversity.

SUDDEN TRANSFORMATION, OR THE GREAT REVERSALS

Christianity's sudden transformation was not predicted by anyone, except for possibly Lesslie Newbigin, David Barrett, and Walbert Bühlmann.[3] Many scholars are now trying to make sense of what happened after the collapse of colonialism and the rise of new African

---

[3]See Lesslie Newbigin, *The Household of God: Lectures on the Nature of the Church* (London: SCM Press, 1953; repr., Eugene, OR: Wipf & Stock, 2008), where he already described Pentecostal Christianity as one of four major forms of Christianity, when many mainline Christians were hoping it would just go away; David Barrett, "AD 2000: 350 Million Christians in Africa," *International Review of Mission* 59, no. 233 (January 1970): 39; and Bühlmann's *The Coming of the Third Church: An Analysis of the Present and Future of the Church* (Maryknoll, NY: Orbis, 1977), where he recognizes the importance and significance of the rise of non-Western Christianity as it is starting to make its global move.

and Asian nation-states. Postcolonial studies and postmodern studies are both methodologies and strategies for scholarly discourse that have helped to de-center the old Western academic and ecclesial hegemonies. However, making sense of twenty-first-century Christianity is much more complex than simply sitting in a different chair, looking with different eyes, or listening to different accents.

Christianity has contradicted many of our written and unwritten assumptions, and this is why we need more than perspectival revisions. For example, we had assumed that Christianity always flourished *only* with political support or favor. Much early church scholarship still holds onto this assumption, as scholars seek to show that only the government-approved forms of Christianity prevailed, and the (mostly Gnostic) forms that did not win imperial favor were crushed. It was not survival of the fittest or truest, but survival of the politically connected, so they say.[4] Historians writing about the early-modern colonial period also assumed that Christianity spread *because* of its support from the colonial powers. Christianity was forced on India and Rhodesia and the Gold Coast and Mexico. That is why Christianity spread across the world. However, this "coattails" historiography is now being put to rest, since we see now that Christianity is neither so dependent nor tame. Christianity has a life of its own, but what does that mean? And how can we think rationally and faithfully about Christianity with this new understanding?

What is some of the evidence from Christianity today that shows us that our contemporary reductionisms of Christianity ("Christianity is merely the spiritual side of empire") are inadequate and actually highly misleading? Much has been written about this in the past decade or so, but rehearsing some of the disorienting stories will help

---

[4]See for example, Karen L. King, *What Is Gnosticism?* (Cambridge, MA: Harvard University Press, 2003) and Bart D. Ehrman's corpus: *Lost Christianities: The Battles for Scripture and the Faiths We Never Knew* (New York: Oxford University Press, 2003); *Misquoting Jesus: The Story Behind Who Changed the Bible and Why* (New York: HarperSanFrancisco, 2005); *Lost Scriptures: Books That Did Not Make it into the New Testament* (New York: Oxford University Press, 2003).

to focus the following chapters.[5] Here I offer three remarkable transformations of Christianity.

The first and greatest transformation is Africa. Lamin Sanneh, in
his creative book *Whose Religion Is Christianity?*, lays out the argument very well.[6]

> The current worldwide Christian resurgence has prompted fresh skep-
> ticism across departments, institutions and disciplines, skepticism about
> the nature, scope, outcome, and implications of Christian growth and
> expansion. Many writers argue that we live in a post-Christian West, and
> that, thanks to irreversible secularization, we have outlived the reigning
> convictions of a once Christian society. . . . Such a secular mood swing, we
> are cautioned, does not bode well for the prospects of worldwide Christian
> resurgence being welcome in the West. . . . The contemporary confidence
> in the secular destiny of the West as an elevated stage of human civilization
> is matched by the contrasting evidence of the resurgence of Christianity as
> a world religion; they are like two streams flowing in opposite directions.[7]

Here Sanneh has identified the empirical fact (explosive growth of
Christianity in the non-Western world) and the reigning academic
paradigm (the elevated and inevitable secular destiny of all cultures).
Both are of interest to us, but we want first to look at the "disturbing"
resurgence of Christianity in Africa.[8] A few facts, now commonly
known, should help us see how disturbing this revival of an African
religion (Christianity) really is.[9]

---

[5]Many people have written about the modern rise of global Christianity, but the father of them
all is Andrew Walls, who has been mentor directly or indirectly to many of us. Others who have
contributed a great deal to the modern understanding of worldwide Christianity include Lammin
Sanneh, Brian Stanley, Joel Carpenter, Philip Jenkins, Jehu Hanciles, Dana Robert, and Ogbu
Kalu, among others, and publications like *The World Christian Encyclopedia* and *The Journal of
World Christianity*.
[6]Lamin Sanneh, *Whose Religion Is Christianity? The Gospel Beyond the West* (Grand Rapids, MI:
Eerdmans, 2003).
[7]Sanneh, *Whose Religion Is Christianity?*, 1-3.
[8]Later we look at meaning and the unavoidable and important issues of interpretation *of* history, *through* history.
[9]From Kwame Bediako, *Christianity in Africa: The Renewal of Non-Western Religion* (Maryknoll,
NY: Orbis, 1995).

After centuries of missionary activity and the earlier thriving of two ancient African Christian kingdoms (Nubia and Ethiopia), Christianity in Africa was only about 9 percent of the population, or 8.7 million in 1900.[10] The Muslim population was 400 percent larger in Africa. At the time of decolonialization (1962) there were still only 60 million Christians; this showed some growth, but surprisingly the real growth occurred after the Second World War and *after* colonialism was mostly dismantled. Then, without foreign support or the resources and control of the church, Christianity *grew* from 60 million in 1962 to 120 million in 1970, and the growth continued. Growing at a rate of about 6 million a year in the 1980s, Christianity grew from 120 million in 1970 to 330 million in 1998 and over 350 million in the year 2000.[11] As Lamin Sanneh, Kwame Bediako, Ogbu Kalu, and others have explained it, Christianity affirmed African religious sensitivities and was identified with an Africa freed from Western hegemony.

> Africans embraced Christianity because it resonated so well with the values of the old religions. . . . People sensed in their hearts that Jesus did not mock their respect for the sacred or their clamor for an invincible Savior, and so they beat their sacred drums for him until the stars skipped and danced in the skies. After that dance the stars weren't little anymore. Christianity helped Africans to become renewed Africans, not remade Europeans.[12]

But how did this happen, and how did it happen so quickly? Many African religious historians are clear on the process, even if the details and specific causes are not known. One of the main causes is African agency. African Christian leadership began to rise up in the early decades of the twentieth century, and they seemed quite

---

[10]For a visual representation of this demographic revolution in Africa, see Mark Shaw and Wanjiru M. Gitau, *The Kingdom of God in Africa*, rev. ed. (Carlisle, UK: Langham Global Library, 2020), 3. These statistics and those from Lamin Sanneh come from the work of Todd M. Johnson and Gina A. Zurlo, eds., *World Christian Database* (Boston: Brill, 2021), www .worldchristiandatabase.org.

[11]Sanneh, *Whose Religion Is Christianity?*, 15, 41.

[12]Sanneh, *Whose Religion Is Christianity?*, 43.

prepared to lead the African church. However, most of the twentieth century was marked by cautious to blatant racism in missionary work in Africa. Ogbu Kalu is direct: "Enlargement of scale and other exigencies forced an increased use of indigenous 'resources,' but there was still an unwillingness to ordain and promote Indigenous people. The racist ideology of the period, the control and monopoly of religion, countered the imperatives of the local contexts."[13] When prevented from leading their own religious (Christian) communities, many prophets initiated their own church movements. African Initiated (Indigenous) Churches (AICs) were the result. Christianity began to be expressed as a movement of resistance against colonial and foreign missionary control. We will look later at the growth of these churches, but with decolonialization came revivals in the "mission" churches as well as in the AICs. Part of the answer to our question above is that Christianity grew through resistance to the West—the Christendom West.

Another element of this answer has to do with the translation principle: the simple fact that Christianity at its best is translated into local cultural and social contexts.[14] Even when done poorly, translation means that Jesus Christ is detached from a particular cultural dominance and is free to enter into and lift up each particular culture. In Africa this meant that the name for the triune God was not imported from the West, but a local name for the great Creator God was used and then explained. God became identified with the long cultural history of each indigene. God's words, when translated, were heard as "our words." God spoke Kwaswahili and Igbo; God spoke to the heart language of each indigene.

---

[13]Ogbu U. Kalu, "Changing Tides: Some Currents in World Christianity at the Opening of the Twenty-First Century," in *Interpreting Contemporary Christianity: Global Processes and Local Identities*, ed. Ogbu U. Kalu and Aaline Low (Grand Rapids, MI: Eerdmans, 2008), 16.

[14]The best introductions to this are Lamin Sanneh, *Translating the Message: The Missionary Impact on Culture* (Maryknoll, NY: Orbis, 1989); Steven Bevens, *Models of Contextual Theology*, rev. ed. (Maryknoll, NY: Orbis, 2002).

The second disorienting story about Christianity from the last two generations is that of China and the Chinese diaspora. Christian witness to China goes back to the year 635 when Alopen, a Persian monk and missionary, first arrived in the Tang Dynasty capital of Xian (Chang-an). The story has been told many times how the empire turned against monks (not just Christians), and over the years, Christianity did not seem to survive at all. A second introduction of Christianity occurred (Franciscans) in the thirteenth and fourteenth centuries under the Yuan (Mongol) Dynasty, and a third (Jesuit) came after the Reformation. A fourth introduction came (Protestants and Catholics) in the nineteenth century toward the end of the Qing Dynasty. At the time of the communist "liberation" in China, it was estimated that there were less than two million Christians in China (1949). After thirteen hundred years of Christian witness, less than two million Chinese were Christian.[15]

In the late 1970s, when knowledge about Christianity in China began to seep out, it was discovered by outsiders that Christianity not only survived but thrived as an explosion of hidden Christian growth. Statistics are hard to come by, but one little fact is very telling. There have been over two hundred million Bibles printed in China since the first modern printing at the Nanjing Amity Press began as a joint venture with the United Bible Societies in 1988.[16] But what is of even more interest is that it is not just Chinese in China who are becoming Christian at a very rapid rate.[17] Chinese in Southeast Asia

---

[15]For a brief overview of this transformation see Sunquist, "The Century That Changed the Religious Map," in *Explorations in Asian Christianity: History, Theology and Mission* (Downers Grove, IL: IVP Academic, 2017).

[16]Over 85 million have been distributed in China; the rest were printed in 130 other languages for other nations.

[17]The Christian population of China is unknown for many reasons: the country is very large, many Christians do not want to be known or identified, some "culture Christians" are not baptized (but they read the Bible every day and try to follow Jesus), and the official statistics count only those in the government recognized churches. According to the Chinese government there are 44 million Christians; Pew, 70.9 million; Operation World, 105 million; Johnson and Zurlo (*World Christian Encyclopedia*), 106 million.

(*Nanyang* Chinese) as well as in Australia and Vancouver and on American college campuses are also turning to Christ. We can describe it, but it is much harder to explain using traditional academic theories of Christianity.[18]

Our third disorienting story about contemporary Christianity is a story that is still unfolding and is known by few. This is the story of church growth now occurring in Indochina, Iran, and Nepal. Cambodia, Vietnam, and Laos, former French colonies, have been very resistant to Protestant forms of Christianity, and in fact were resistant to most non-Asian influences for most of the modern world. One of the great stories of faithfulness in mission is that of the Jesuit Alexandre de Rhodes (1593–1660) and his colleagues who carried out Christian witness in Cochinchine and Tonkin in the early seventeenth century. De Rhodes spent as much time in Vietnamese prisons and in exile as he did in missionary work during his twenty years of outreach. And yet with all of the resistance and persecution, the church grew dramatically under Indigenous leadership. Persecution continued and even accelerated during the nineteenth century.

In the modern period, the spread of atheistic communism in Southeast Asia was seen as a new and equally smothering form of persecution for the church. Many of us have met Vietnamese Christian refugees and heard their stories of churches being closed, pastors imprisoned, and some Christians being sent off, never to be heard from again. When Vietnam, in part following the lead of China, began to open its borders to the nations, it was discovered that the church had survived and had even grown. Between 1967 and 2005 the smaller of the two major churches, the Protestant Church in Vietnam, had grown between eight- and tenfold.[19] Most of the church growth is taking place

---

[18]Chinese in China are also turning back to (or rediscovering) Buddhism, but this is what one might expect after two millennia of Buddhist presence in China.

[19]According to Johnson and Zurlo, church growth in Vietnam has been dramatic: 1970, 3.3 million; 2000, 6.5 million; 2015, 8 million; 2020, 8.9 million.

by Vietnamese evangelists and pastors aided by other Asian Christians from countries like Malaysia, Taiwan, Hong Kong, Singapore, and even Indonesia and China. Cambodia has had an even more difficult time developing a viable Indigenous church, and yet in the past two decades Asian Christians have developed Methodist, Anglican, Presbyterian, Pentecostal, and other churches in Cambodia with very little involvement from the West. These Asian missionaries are running training centers, schools, and orphanages in addition to planting churches.

Nepal, a Hindu kingdom, has been one of the most difficult countries in the world in which to carry out Christian witness. It was not until 1990 that the ban on political parties was lifted and a new constitution was passed. After a slow opening to the world in 1951, when Christian groups could enter for humanitarian but not religious work, a few missions began to take up residence in the country. For nearly forty years little overt Christian witness was possible. Today, however, due to well-seasoned Indigenous leaders, many trained in India, and other Asian missionaries, Christianity is developing as a South Asian religion. Estimates are hard to come by, but it seems that there are over 1.3 million Christians in a country that could count only 30,000 Christians in 1991. The annual growth rate of the Protestant Christian community in Nepal in 2000 was over 25 percent.[20] As Lamin Sanneh says, "No amount of institution organizing can cope with the momentum" of church growth outside the West.[21] These movements of contemporary Christianity have proven to be unwieldy for Western institutions, including Western theology. This is part of what Andrew Walls was saying in January 2010.

All of these examples are the tip of the global Christian iceberg; a massive, powerful, moving entity that appears serene and insignificant

[20]Cindy Perry, "Nepal," in *A Dictionary of Asian Christianity*, ed. Scott W. Sunquist, David Wu Chu Sing, and John Chew Hiang Chia (Grand Rapids, MI: Eerdmans, 2001), 593-95; "Nepal," in *Operation World*, ed. Jason Mandryk (Downers Grove, IL: InterVarsity Press, 2021).

[21]Sanneh, *Whose Religion Is Christianity?*, 3.

on top but has power to bring down the greatest and most respected theories and theologies. We can no longer evaluate global Christianity as a younger (or similar) form of Western Christianity. Chinese Christianity is developing within the soil of Confucian and even socialist nutrients as Western Christianity developed in the soil of Greek and Latin nutrients. African Independent Churches are developing as African religions that happen to be Christian—even though a Presbyterian from Peoria may see these churches as heretical or unhealthily syncretistic. These movements are not traversing the same path we in the West trod. We should not wait for them to "grow up" and become domesticated like Western Christianity. These are movements that have different histories, different contexts, and different trajectories than Western Christianity. They cannot be studied as if they are younger versions of us. Many of these non-Western movements have no knowledge of a European Reformation or of the Council of Nicea. These are first- or second-century churches that have begun in the twentieth or twenty-first century. Their process of development and the contemporary globalized context is not what the Western church experienced, but they all share the same origins. If we read them as "like us only younger," we are misreading these movements and will therefore miss the lessons we could learn about Christianity. But, we might ask, if they are so different, and they have their own integrity and must be judged on their own merits, what do we really share in common? Maybe we should accept the new vocabulary of many different Christianities. Maybe these are actually new religions related to Christianity. After all, what does Athens have to do with Accra?

CHRISTIANITY AND WORLD CHRISTIANITIES

With such diversity to Christianity today, or at least with much greater awareness of such diversity, scholars struggle to make sense of Christianity. The "norm" is no longer the norm. Basic assumptions about Christianity no longer hold. Therefore we either have to recalibrate how we understand Christianity as a movement in history (what this volume is about), or we reinvent Christianity as various movements or even religions that all have a common heritage—a shared early myth—but not a common center today. The question of center and boundaries is an important one, and one we deal with throughout this volume. At this point we simply want to say that the choice of a new understanding of Christianity's DNA is one option for making sense of the above changes. The other choice that has begun to emerge is simply to say that Christianity is not one at all but rather diverse movements with some shared symbols. One Christianity or many? That is the question.[22]

Many scholars, institutions, and publishers are now finding it easier to talk about the many *Christianities* in the world rather than talking about the diversity of expressions of Christianity. Here are some quick examples and an explanation of why it is a problem. The impressive new Cambridge series, *Cambridge History of Christianity* (in nine volumes), decided to express the new situation of Christianity in the world by resorting to the plural in its last two volumes. The first seven volumes, covering up to the nineteenth century, do not use the plural, even though they cover the great diversity of Christianity, such as crusading Christianity, East Syrian (dyophysite or "Nestorian") Christianity, apocalyptic movements, Roman Catholic persecutions of Protestants, and more. It is only when they begin to talk about the growth of Christianity in Africa and Asia in the modern world that the volumes begin to talk about Christianity in the plural (volumes 8–9). Does this mean that Christianity became different religions once it broke out of its Western forms (some might say prison)? It can look like Western scholars have a hard time seeing the new global expression of Christianity as part of "their" Christianity, so they have to call it a different Christianity.

---

[22]See also Scott Sunquist, "World Christianity: Transforming Church History and Theology," in *Explorations in Asian Christianity*, 143–64.

Some universities now have chairs in world Christianities rather than world Christianity.[23] Once again, including more non-Western sources and stories is an indicator that Christianity has become different religions. Other publications are beginning to talk about Christianities when they talk about the non-Western world. Heather Sharkey from the University of Pennsylvania has written a fascinating article about a Muslim convert from Egypt who became a missionary doctor in China.[24] Wipf and Stock has also accepted the new designation, having pioneered a series called "Studies in the History of Culture and of World Christianities." Philip Jenkins talks about the "modern-day rise of world Christianities" when endorsing Alister McGrath's *Christianity's Dangerous Idea*. Peter Phan talks about Asian Christianities in his Edward Cadbury lectures.[25]

Then conferences of scholars began to talk about Christianity in the plural. In April 2010 there was a conference held in Edinburgh on the "Changing Face of Christianity." In the description of the conference we read, "World Christianities are increasingly influential, and migration and diaspora Christianities are (re)-shaping Christianity in the West." Here again only when we move outside of the norm (West) does Christianity fragment into many different religions. In all of our examples the West is still represented as having a monolithic Christianity.

Finally, with publications, academic chairs, and conferences talking about non-Western Christianity in the plural, there will be courses offered that designate Christianity in the plural (when it is

[23]Perkins School of Theology at Southern Methodist University is one. Drew University has initiated a new center, the Drew Center for Christianities in Global Context. Christianity is plural, but there is a single global context. The University of Chicago has a new chair in Global Christianity. The University of Birmingham (England) also has a new chair in world Christianity, as does Baylor University in Texas. The University of Cambridge has world Christianities as an area of research, including an explanation for the use of the plural; see "World Christianities," www.divinity.cam.ac.uk/researchareas/research-areas/wc#section-3.

[24]Heather Sharkey, "An Egyptian in China: Ahmed Fahmy and the Making of World Christianities," *Church History* 78, no. 2 (2009): 309-26.

[25]Peter Phan, *Asian Christianities: History, Theology, Practice* (Maryknoll, NY: Orbis, 2018).

non-Western).[26] One such course is Global Christianity in Modern Historical Perspectives. In the course description we read:

> The aim of this course is to help students appreciate the present profession of World Christianities, the commonalities that draw them together and the differences that divide them. . . . The present profusion and diversity of Christian movements raises the question of whether there is any identifiable traits or set of traits that could allow us to identify a religious movement as "Christian," and if not, whether we should henceforth speak of Christianities.[27]

These and many other examples show how we are beginning to accept a new vocabulary about Christianity to make sense (as Western scholars) of something that is beyond our framework or mindset, and something that was certainly beyond our expectation. We have a religion which we call Christianity, but now that we no longer have hegemony or linguistic control over the movement (not that we ever did), we can only make sense of these new expressions by calling them something different. Christianity is no longer one religion. It has become many different religions outside of its Western hegemony.

If we are so quick to let go of the thread that holds Christianity together, it seems we will have other problems. Can we even define Christianity today?[28] Churches and ecumenical agencies must, and they do. They may err in drawing the line at times (excluding some for racial, political, or economic reasons), and yet it is necessary to see that there is a difference between Methodist and Mormon or Jesus People USA and Jehovah's Witnesses. Under the new Christianities,

---

[26]See for example Cambridge University, "World Christianities Research Seminar," www.divinity.cam.ac.uk/researchareas/seminars/world-christianities.

[27]Brian Clark, Global Christianity in Modern Historical Perspectives, course taught at Hartford Seminary, Winter 2009.

[28]My earlier description of what elements are essential to Christian coherence: "Christian coherence is found in that Christians, in all their diverse beliefs and practices, find their identity in Jesus Christ, they look to the Scriptures to explain who he is and who they are to be, as they gather to remember, honor, and spread the teachings and practices that Jesus commends, and they are aware that God is somehow active through his Spirit in what they do and say." Sunquist, *Explorations in Asian Christianity*, 161.

what is to prevent us from including Sung Yung Moon's Unification Church as one of the new forms of Christianity? Such an inclusion would go beyond what Asian Christians would approve and even what as inclusive an ecumenical body as the World Council of Churches would accept. Christianity must be something and not everything. There is a philosophy of history or theology behind such a change, and the following pages are written in part to challenge this popular academic trend. Behind all of this discussion is the call to make proper judgments regarding issues, beliefs, and movements. In chapter four and the epilogue of this book we will look at discernment, or what the ancients call "discrimination," an important theme in making sense of history.

Rather than jettison twenty centuries of Christian identity ("one holy, catholic and apostolic church"), we offer a more radical (*radix*, "root") solution. The Jesus movement that is rooted in the birth, life, suffering, death, resurrection, and ascension of Jesus Christ is a single movement called Christianity. It is not only possible but necessary to understand this movement as rooted in the person and work of Jesus Christ. Nothing is more fundamental. When it moves off that foundation or center it is no longer Christianity but rather a new loyalty that might use more or less of the teachings and stories of Jesus Christ. It is important to be able to identify the difference between the two. It is not only permissible but also necessary to humbly and carefully draw the lines. At times it is hard to know, but it is important to critique expressions of Christianity that are less Christian (e.g., the use of violence to bring about conversion) from those that are more Christian (laying down your life for your friends). How can we do that without denying our own particular religious heritage or without becoming so generic that in the end we have said nothing? We can only do this from the evidence of Christianity expressed as the Great Tradition through twenty centuries and throughout the whole globe. We cannot say anything universal about Christianity if we write only from our own tradition (small "t") or from our own cultural or political context. This was very common in the past with the writing of "ecclesiastical histories," which were written as apologetic arguments against Anabaptists, Roman Catholics, Protestants, and so on. Listening to the whole church through all the ages is a prerequisite to our project. Thus the importance of "world" Christianity for this new understanding of the Jesus movement.

CHRISTIAN MOVEMENT AS HISTORY AND FAITH

These chapters, therefore, try to make sense of the new global Christian movement as a historical movement with a common DNA, with ligaments and sinews holding it all together as a single body of Christ, the coming kingdom of God. We want to understand this for the sake of historical and theological study of Christianity today. But we also want to understand this more accurately for the sake of the future. Historical studies should always have the future in view. These chapters seek to understand better the following compound question: *What is Christianity as a historical movement, and how can we best understand and explain Christianity as God's redemptive work in history?* Please note that this compound question—focusing on a *historical* movement linked to the *faith* commitment that in Christianity we see something of God's redemptive work—is being asked on the other side of modernity. This means we are studying Christianity on its own terms or according to its own faith commitment. In 2 Corinthians 5:19 we read, "In Christ God was reconciling the world to himself, not counting their trespasses against them, and entrusting the message of reconciliation to us." Scripture claims that it is in Jesus Christ, the historic figure who lived in the Middle East, that a cosmic work was and is being done: the world is being reconciled to God. The full meaning of this is expressed throughout Scripture, but this global, even cosmic work of reconciliation (also redemption, liberation, healing) is the lens that should focus the study of Christian history as we study it on its own terms.[29]

Scholarly neutrality is a myth that guided Enlightenment scholarship, but we still find that many scholars try to work with the assumption that we can be purely rational and scientific about the study of human cultures and behaviors (including religion). Historical studies involve faith just as much as the studies of economics, sociology, or psychology. The Jesuit historian M. C. D'Arcy expressed with lucid candor the nature of historical studies in contrast to the studies of modern science as described before the Second World War. In the volume *The Sense of History: Secular and Sacred* that came from his 1938 lectures given to the Oxford Society of Historical Theology, he summarizes these issues for us in the following manner: "One is that history differs from science, and is none the worse for that. Secondly, history is concerned with the particular or quasi-particular in contrast to science which is satisfied with types. Thirdly, history uses interpretation; it seeks for an intelligible pattern or whole."[30]

This quotation reveals an earlier distinction between types of study: hard science deals with "types" and facts. History (and presumably psychology) looks for patterns in the particular events in time. This academic dichotomy is challenged today with various interdisciplinary studies and with the newer concept of "intellectual humility."[31] Intellectual humility posits that siloed disciplines of study prevent rather than promote true knowledge and learning. It takes humility to

---

[29]Studying the development of a vaccine to fight Covid-19 also comes to mind. Such a historical study, done on its own terms, would focus on decisions made, monies raised, directions of the research, and so on. It is possible that some research firms were more focused on political advantage or profit than in actually serving humanity. Studying the development on its own terms (how institutions made decisions to end the pandemic) will reveal false as well as true motives. Were the researchers and the pharmaceutical companies true to their stated purposes, or were they driven by ulterior motives and purposes?

[30]M. C. D'Arcy, SJ, *The Sense of History: Secular and Sacred* (London: Faber and Faber, 1959), 23.

[31]See Brian Resnick, "Intellectual Humility: The Importance of Knowing You Might Be Wrong," Vox.com, January 4, 2019, www.vox.com/science-and-health/2019/1/4/17989224/intellectual-humility-explained-psychology-replication.

admit that my discipline needs to learn from those in other disciplines. The historian knows that she needs to ask for the help of economists, psychologists, and sociologists to explain events and decisions of the past. Putting an end to a pandemic is not just a matter of studying infectious diseases; it involves politics, communications, psychology, and economics (and much more). Knowledge is a connected matrix of disciplines, not siloed depositories of facts.

Thus, the historian is concerned with multiple causes and motives, and then searches for "intelligible patterns." Every historian must make sense of the various forms of data or evidence that she or he gathers. Making sense of it involves meaning. We come with preliminary understandings and commitments, and then we allow the evidence to sharpen or further shape our understandings. From the start we need to know what questions to ask. What is the subject we are studying, and how do we question the evidence? Historical work, as we can see, starts with an awareness of our present contexts and commitments. Each of us has commitments and assumptions we hope are more liberating than binding, more general than specific. As a historian of Christianity and a Christian historian I hope that my commitment as a Christian is stronger than my commitment as a Presbyterian. I also hope that my commitment as a Christian is stronger than my commitment as an American citizen. Other historian friends of mine start as Reformed Afrikaners or Kachin Baptists, but they still need to study Christianity as global citizens and as Christians more than as Reformed South Africans or as Baptists in Myanmar.

Our compound question highlighted above has two lines of vision. How we answer this compound question will have both a pedagogical line of development and a practical line. It will influence how we research, teach, and live. How we understand Christianity as a movement in history will determine how we teach it, how we prepare students to live in new globalized world, how we prepare pastors, and how we equip missionaries. What do we focus on, and what do we leave out?

What are we looking for in our research? The art of the historian is mostly a matter of doing extensive research and then deciding what to leave out, so how we answer this question will help us in the art of historical excising.

Thus, our question has both ethical and moral dimensions to it.[32] I come from a long line of teachers, and having majored in education decades ago, I still am aware of the truth that education is not a neutral science. It is a moral as well as political act to educate. To educate is to lead (*educo*: "to lead out"), and leading involves clear direction, responsible work, and accountability. Jesus talks about the misuse of pedagogy resulting in having a millstone strung around your neck and being thrown in a lake. Jesus, Marx, and politicians running for office all realized that education is a moral undertaking. Minds can be corrupted or corrected; lives can be saved or starved by teachers and scholars. In universities and seminaries, we are often so far removed from the "end product" (pastor applying the Word to a family's life) that we seldom recognize our responsibility and accountability. I believe that how we answer this question has moral, ethical, and political implications. It would be much easier if our historical and theological scholarship could be as neutral as it was once thought to be. However, historians have recognized for over half a century that neutrality in history is neither possible nor desirable.[33] Georges Florovsky noted in 1959, "The point is that even a pretended neutrality, and alleged freedom from bias, is itself a bias, an option, a decision. In fact, again contrary to the current prejudice, commitment is a token of freedom, a prerequisite of responsiveness. Concern and interest imply commitment."[34]

---

[32]See, for example, Oliver O'Donovan, *The Ways of Judgment* (Grand Rapids, MI: Eerdmans, 2005), esp. 3-12.

[33]See C. H. McIlwain, A. Myendorf, and J. L. Morrison, "Bias in Historical Writing," *History* 11, no. 43 (1926): 193-203.

[34]Georges Florovsky, "The Predicament of the Christian Historian," in *God, History, and Historians: An Anthology of Modern Christian Views of History*, ed. C. T. McIntire (New York: Oxford University Press, 1977), 427.

History is a constructive and formative art. When we teach history, we are directing the minds and affections of students, and we are building an image of the church.

This may seem like an odd way of framing the question, so let me explain. I mentioned that two long projects have shaped my thinking about history. A number of years ago I presented a premature paper on the meaning of Christian history and the writing of Christian history while working on volume two of *History of the World Christian Movement.* The paper was to be an introduction or epilogue (I am often not sure whether I am coming or going) for the volume.[35] It was a well-researched paper tracing historiography in the past two centuries that timidly worked toward the conclusion that all of nineteenth- and twentieth-century historiography was leading to our book. The paper was not only premature; it was also self-serving. It deserved to be ignored even though it was heavily researched. However, my bad paper and everyone else's evening was redeemed by an insightful question from a South African ethicist. "Scott, you have been reading about church history globally for the past ten years or so. Few people are forced to read so widely about Christian history: the Pacific and Potomac, the Balkans and Batakland, and of course Pretoria and Princeton. You have had to tell all of this as a single story, to make some sense of various movements as all part of the fabric of Christianity. Tell us, what have you learned?"

It was not the question I was expecting. With his question he graciously swept my paper from our gaze and put on the table something much more solid, precious, and important: the question of meaning, if not of purpose, in historical writing. On one hand I was in shock. On the other hand, it was a very simple question to answer. "What I have learned is that Christianity is so fragile, but powerful enough to change the world." That is it.

---

[35]Dale Irvin and Scott Sunquist, *History of the World Christian Movement*, vol. 2 , *Modern Christianity from 1454 to 1800* (Maryknoll, NY: Orbis, 2012).

As I explained this, scenarios from across the centuries and across the seas came to my mind. These scenes all revealed something of the missional meaning or the missional trajectory of Christianity. Christianity—even under terrible conditions or with uneducated leaders—is constantly moving out. But as it moves out, it transforms cultures. As I was concluding my brief exposition, an image came to mind that I will stick with and that I want to stick with you. Christianity is a thin, red thread woven into the fabric of history that has changed the world. The thin, red thread is the message of Christianity. Christianity is not primarily about buildings, institutions, or worldly power. It is fairly simple; it is about a transformative message. It does not have to be written; in fact it is usually just spoken. What could be more exposed and fragile? The message spoken is something like this: "God created all things, and in Jesus Christ he came to forgive sin and to show us how to live. His message was rejected; he was killed on the cross and buried. He rose from the dead, and now through his Holy Spirit, he continues his work of liberation and redemption through the church."

We may quibble with some of the words here, but this is the basic message that is proclaimed in the sacred liturgies of the East and by Pentecostal evangelists and is the source material for some of the greatest Western literature. It has been translated, spoken, acted out, sung, preached, and danced, and through this message people and their cultures have been transformed. Lives have been saved and sacrificed around this message. At the heart of Christianity, as it has been expressed and as it has developed in the world, is a thin, red thread.

During the past few years, I have expanded that simple image into three concepts of time, cross, and glory. The thin red thread involves three strands, woven together, which mark Christianity as Christianity. The first thread is the concept of time. Whether it is the Gospel of John or the first letter of John, Christianity is a religion rooted in, even one that introduces the concept of, time. In the first two chapters we develop this idea as a unique contribution of Christianity to world understanding and knowledge, but we also show what it means in identifying Christianity and seeing the contrast with its imitators. Time implies movement, whether it be interpreted as development/advancement or devolution/decline. Time, as we have it expressed in Christianity, also has a beginning, an end, and a center. This leads us to the second concept.

The cross is the second concept or strand. The cross here symbolizes the central, historic event of Christianity (found in time) and the source of the Christian life. We expand the concept from cross as symbol of suffering and sacrifice to the larger concept of the cruciform and apostolic nature of Christianity.[36] Chapter three develops this concept of cross and apostolic identity in Christian history and shows how it takes on local contexts and then transforms them.

The fourth chapter develops the third characteristic of Christianity as a historic movement, the concept of future glory. Possibly out of fear of steering glory too far to the present and developing a triumphalistic Christianity, and on the other side interpreting Christianity as only a future glory and therefore ignoring present secular realities, this concept has not been given its due in the study of Christian history. Glory (and the closely related concept of joy) is a central concept to Christianity, and it has been and should be understood as the important third of the three strands of the thin red thread. The volume concludes with some ideas of what this understanding of Christianity as a movement in history should mean for the study of history as well as for Christian life today.

How to Use This Volume

This volume is not a church history book, but it is about church history. It is not a missiology book, but it guides us in how we should study

---

[36]See Scott Sunquist, "Missio Dei: Christian History Envisioned as Cruciform Apostolicity," *Missiology* 37, no. 1 (2009): 33-46.

the mission of the church. This is not a book on world Christianity, but the examples and the genesis of the book come from the study of world Christianity. Finally, this is not a book on Christian theology, but it should initiate some discussions on how theology needs to think differently about essential tenets and how they should be expressed for our global church today.

This book is an introduction to the writing and study of Christian history and the mission of the church in light of the great reversals of the last decades of the twentieth century. It is offered as a way to help students of Christianity understand how to study Christianity as a historical movement in light of the great transformations suggested above. So many of the assumptions that drove the greatest of Western historians and theologians in the past have to be revised, and therefore the studies that follow from these assumptions will also need to be reworked on the global academic stage. It is not being honest before the newer global realities to assume that Christianity survives or thrives when it has proper support from governments or from economic patrons. Neither is it being honest before the global church to develop a systematic theology that assumes medieval European categories. And (much to my chagrin) it is not true that if we just get the theology right, the church will be healthy and grow.

When we hold on to these false assumptions about the past, we have obscured something of Christianity, and on other occasions we have excluded much that was Christian in cultures not our own. How we envision and study Christianity can enlighten and liberate, but it can also obscure and misjudge other Christians. When this happens, we have misunderstood Christianity. We want here to understand something of the essence of Christianity as it has been handed down and as it was (we believe) first understood by those closest to the foundations. Thus, we frequently refer to the New Testament, the earliest interpreters of the Scriptures, and the Jesus movement, and then look around the world and across the centuries. Again, in this sense what follows is a radical study of Christianity as a movement in history, which makes sense from beginning (its genesis) to the end (eschaton).

It is hoped that a student beginning her or his study of Christianity, either in a university or a Christian academic setting, will better understand this global movement on its own terms. Thus, this is a foundational book. This is an introductory book based on the study of Christianity through its twenty centuries of history, its global expressions, and from personal experience in North America, Africa, Europe, and Asia.

As much as any religion and more than most, Christianity is a religion of history, rooted in historic events and a full participant in this world. Christianity is deeply historical and secular.[37] Thus, to understand Christianity, a person must be, at least on one level, a type of historian. This does not mean that creedal statements are mere listings of facts, but they are historical statements that are part of the Christian story.

No chronicle is history. In the sharp phrase of Benedetto Croce, a chronicle is but a "corpse of history": *il cadavere*. A chronicle is but a thing (*una cosa*), a complex of sounds and other signs. But history is "an act of the spirit," *un atto spirituale.*[38]

I would say that history is also a story above all. It is millions of stories, but it is also a story; it must be learned as a narrative for it to make sense and for it to be instructive. What follows is a guide through the great tropical jungle of *Christian* history—a jungle that at times seems foreign, chaotic, and meaningless, but it has its own meaning and ecosystem and its own vital spirit.

---

[37]I use the word *secular* here as it has been used in the church (in Latin: *saeculum*) for "this age" or for "the world." Most religions are not so "secular," meaning rooted in and expressed in and for this world. Christianity is not an escapist religion but a religion that is for the world.
[38]Florovsky, "Predicament of the Christian Historian," 313.

Chapter One

A Brief History of History

He has made everything suitable for its time; moreover he has put a sense of past and future into their minds, yet they cannot find out what God has done from the beginning to the end.

ECCLESIASTES 3:11

In the beginning was the Word, and the Word was with God, and the Word was God. He was in the beginning with God. All things came into being through him, and without him not one thing came into being. What has come into being in him was life, and the life was the light of all people. . . . And the Word became flesh and lived among us.

JOHN 1:1-4, 14

We declare to you what was from the beginning, what we have heard, what we have seen with our eyes, what we have looked at and touched with our hands, concerning the word of life—this life was revealed, and we have seen it and testify to it, and declare to you the eternal life that was with the Father and was revealed to us—we declare to you what we have seen and heard so that you also may have fellowship with us; and truly our fellowship is with the Father and with his Son Jesus Christ.

1 JOHN 1:1-3

CHRISTIANITY IS ROOTED IN TIME: historic events in a particular place that have universal claim. Past events have present realities and a future life. People who come from Hellenistic, Hindu, Buddhist, or various animistic religious backgrounds are shocked by the challenge this is to their reigning assumptions. Here the mundane is sacralized, the cyclical is given direction (and meaning), and all people are given equal status. A value and sacredness is assigned to all of creation in a world where most religions devalue the created world. Those who believed in a life of endless rebirths—a cycle they sought to be released from—now have their life focused on this life and the fullness of this life (in time) for all of eternity. Was all of this done in a simple passage like, "And the Word became flesh"? Yes. The incarnation, the translation of God into human flesh, brought about the conversion of humanity and human cultures.

In this chapter, we will lift up something that has been lost or nearly forgotten concerning Christianity and Christian history. To put it simply, we have forgotten that the dual fact of God's creation (beginning time) and God's incarnation (entering time) has been the central strand in what makes Christianity what it is: a religion of transformation in this world. These dual facts also claim to be the interpretive key for all of life.

In answering the compound question mentioned in the introduction —the question about the meaning of the Christian movement and the meaning of God's redemptive work in history—I will first set the context. Princeton Theological Seminary's Students' Lectures on Missions given over the past 120 years provide a convenient context. I will use the history of these lectures as my canvas, and some of the early speakers, especially James Dennis, for my paint. After looking at how Christianity was understood in its historical and cultural context of the early twentieth century, we will turn to look at history from two angles of view. First, we will look at the study of history in the recent past. What is the historian actually doing, or what does the historian think she or he is doing? This will be a much-too-brief look at the development of history writing in the past century, but it will help to set the context for the rest of the book.

Our second angle of view will be covered in the next chapter. In chapter two we will look at the overall concept of history and time and its relationship to redemption. Christianity is very much about time! Christianity did not invent time, but it certainly did make it what it is today. The results of this view of the cosmos will be shown through examples of church history . . . through time. But now, a brief history of history.

HISTORY AND THE LECTURES

James Dennis's three-volume *Christian Missions and Social Progress*[1] is an excellent case study in contextualization and historical understanding. Dennis, a Presbyterian missionary to Syria and historian of missions, gave the first Students' Lecture on Missions, later published as *Foreign Missions After a Century*. In fact, he also gave the fourth lectures, which were later expanded into the massive three-volume work, *Christian Missions and Social Progress*. I will use his understanding of mission and the Christian movement as a starting point. He was not an eccentric or marginal figure by any stretch of the imagination. His views may seem so strange and optimistic to us today, so imperialistic and arrogant, and yet his idea of progress was as natural and common in his time as our commonly held ideas that technology holds the answers for the future, or that pluralism is a virtue. Dennis was a nineteenth-century progressive evangelical rooted in the American Protestant tradition, the confidence of the Student Volunteer Movement, and the sense of duty that was at times expressed as the "white man's burden."[2] The phrase "progressive evangelical"

---

[1] James Dennis, *Christian Missions and Social Progress: A Sociological Study of Foreign Missions*, 3 vols. (New York: Fleming H. Revell, 1897–1906).
[2] This expression was made famous by Rudyard Kipling in his poem "White Man's Burden: The United States and the Philippine Islands," 1899. His intent was to encourage the United States to

makes perfect sense when talking about American Christianity a century ago.

In the introduction to his first volume of *Social Progress* he notes the following:

> That there is a striking apologetic import to the aspect of missions herein presented is evident. It is not merely a vindication of the social value of mission work, but it becomes, in proportion to the reality and significance of the facts put in evidence, a present-day supplement to the cumulative argument of history in defense of Christianity as a supreme force in the social regeneration and elevation of the human race.[3]

His view is illustrated in the wealth of facts, stories, and pictures that fill the volume. For Dennis the missionary message is for "worldwide reformation . . . or . . . regeneration." Listen to his evaluation of history and reform:

> We have had local reformations in religious history; we had them in Hebrew history, before the coming of Christ. The result of early Christian labors was the conversion of the Roman Empire, and in the 16th century came the great historic Reformation of Europe. Now, for the first time in the history of our earth, this great movement in the direction of regeneration or refor-mation is beginning to shape itself into a *world-wide enterprise*.

The sixteenth-century Reformation was only in Europe; thus he says, "May we not expect that a reformation so extended as that contemplated in modern missions will produce world-wide fruit, *especially since it has all the advantages afforded by modern inventions, and facilities and methods of communication, and international relations and the almost magical expedients for disseminating knowledge?*"[4] He and his age had

---

follow Great Britain in becoming colonialists, accepting the burden of taking care of the "half devil, half child." It is a very racist and colonialist rendition of history.

[3]James Dennis, *Christian Missions and Social Progress: A Sociological Study of Foreign Missions* (New York: Fleming H. Revell, 1899), 1:ix. Although assuming "the white man's burden" of lifting up other less-civilized peoples, Dennis uses "race" of all peoples as a uniting word.

[4]Dennis, *Christian Missions and Social Progress*, 2:18. (All emphases, unless otherwise specified, are mine.)

great trust in technology and human inventions. This is what gives him confidence in Christian mission. I don't believe we are that different today, although we will express it differently (stopping climate change, etc.). His views, however, were not yet chastened by the world wars and genocides of the twentieth century. In the preface to volume three he notes, referring to his previous lectures,

> It has been asserted, for example, that missions are a forceful dynamic power in social progress, a molding influence upon *national life*, and a factor of importance in *commercial expansion*, as well as a stimulus to the *religious reformation* not only of *individual lives*, but of *society* as a whole, through many and *varied channels of influence*.[5]

What may cause us to pause is his seemingly imperialistic view of Christianity ("national life, commercial expansion") that sounds like a domination of the world by Christian cultures and nations. He is expressing here a very liberal view of the missionary enterprise, a view that included much more than making converts and planting churches. This was a broad social mission that embraced the core of the gospel and its many products. Dropping the paternalism, it would still seem that the evangelization of cultures or penetration of Christian values of justice and peace is something we should affirm. Jesus' life and death were not just a privatized act for our own self-improvement. They were identification with the lost, lonely, and oppressed in order to usher in new relationships and life called a kingdom. The problem with Dennis from our perspective is not how expansive his vision of mission was but how it was woven with national aspirations and reliance on human efforts (including technology and empire). His interpretation wove nationalism and modern science into his interpretation of God's kingdom coming to earth as it is in heaven.

Dennis was not unique or strange in this view. I cannot emphasize enough that this was the common understanding of Western nations

---

[5]Dennis, *Christian Missions and Social Progress*, 3:v.

and Western theologians, even, or especially, the more progressive of
the time. When we say "all Western nations," this would include
France. In 1899, Dennis was working on his magnum opus as the
Ottoman Empire was collapsing and France, England, and Russia
were moving into the Middle East. With the expanding influence of
the French Empire, the opportunity came for the Benedictines to re-
build a crusader church in Palestine. In a September 11, 1899, letter
from D. Drouhin, OAB (Ordem dos Advogados do Brasil), to French
Consul Ernest Auzépy, we read the following:

> In this surprising concourse of circumstances, there is for us, Mr. Consul,
> a very precious encouragement: we would gladly say, with our generous
> Crusaders of the 11th and 12th century: God wants it. God wants it! Espe-
> cially as our consciences and our hearts give their testimony that, like
> them, we are only *looking for the greatness of our dear France and the
> extension of God's reign,* which for individuals and for peoples is the real,
> the unique source of civilization and happiness.[6]

Our Presbyterian James Dennis is much less imperialistic and nationalistic than the good French Benedictine brother, but that should give
us little solace. Empires were *Christian* empires, and they were all
bestowing their "blessings" on the ignorant and "pagan" countries of
the world. Rebuilding a crusaders' church was understood as part of
the process of bringing "civilization and happiness" to the Middle East.

TIME: ADVANCES AND RECESSIONS

Dennis and Drouhin, and for that matter other great Christian leaders
of the early twentieth century such as John R. Mott, Robert E. Speer,
and Samuel Zwemer, viewed Christianity through their cultural
lenses, and they saw progress—social progress, in fact. Christianity

---

[6]Dominique Trimbur, "Between Eastern and Western Christendom: The Benedictines, France
and the Syrian Catholic Church in Jerusalem," in *Christianity in the Middle East: Studies in Modern
History, Theology and Politics,* ed. Anthony O' Mahony (London: Melisende, 2008), 379. The cry
of the people when Pope Urban II called for the first crusade was *"Deus vult!"* or "God wills it!"

was advancing and bringing with it a better life for all, a life for the West African or Chinese that would be like the best of Western civilization. This basic view was a scholarly or academic view—the view of the academy—but it was also the Fundamentalist and the Pentecostal view of Christianity. The great historian Kenneth Scott Latourette reflected a similar view a half a century later, although he was more chastened by the long historical record he traced. Still, he saw each advance of Christianity as progressing a little further and each recession receding a little less. In his remarkable preface to volume one of *A History of Christianity*, Latourette clearly outlines eight periods of church history, and he does so looking at the advance and recession of the religion and its overall influence on the world's cultures. His last period was not yet complete (1914–1953), but he gives characteristics. He said that even with the "colossal setbacks and striking losses," Christianity was "becoming really worldwide . . . and it is more potent than in any earlier era." He was either an eternal optimist, or he was very prophetic, for the great Christian movement into Africa and Asia was only beginning when he penned those words. He knew of dying Christendom ("what was once termed Christendom") in Europe in the shadow of the two world wars and the rise of atheistic communism, and yet he pronounced the body healthy.[7] He never predicted, nor did any other historian, the rapid decline of Western Christianity that was a reverse image of the non-Western world. Optimism, progressivism, and human ability were themes in the historical writing of Christianity of the period. It was easy for them to see the kingdom of God revealed in modern technology, Christian empires, the missionary movement, new schools, and modern-looking hospitals in poor countries.

All of these historians were telling a story of Christianity as it was unfolding around them in ways that made sense to them and to their

---

[7]Kenneth Scott Latourette, *A History of Christianity*, vol. 1, *Beginnings to 1500* (New York: Harper and Row, 1953), xxi–xxiv.

cultures. This should make us very cautious, careful, and circumspect in our task here. The cultural norms and values can enhance one's historic vision, but they can also obscure both how the story is told and how we understand Christianity. Those telling the story that I have looked at above, and those who spoke in lectureships at Princeton or who taught at Yale, were top scholars, and they were very well informed about Christian history and Christian "progress." The best and the brightest were caught up in contemporary visions of reality that obscured their Christian view of time.

We now live in a new century, and it is necessary to re-center or re-view Christianity today as we understand it in historical perspective. In light of the presence of Christianity today as mostly a non-Western religion (roughly two-thirds), and in light of the errors of the past in equating human technology, social progress, and empire with Christian mission, meaning must now come out of three sources, or must heed three voices. To stick with the analogy of a thread, history must be told by weaving together three strands: the biblical story, the experience of the global church, and its founder. It would be good to reread that last sentence before you go on: biblical story, global church, and Jesus. These three voices or threads will help prevent us from repeating the imperialistic and ethnocentric histories of the past.

None of our great standards for guiding us in our understanding Christian history in the past will work today. We cannot rely on Wesley's quadrilateral (Scripture, tradition, experience, and reason), the Reformation cry of *sola Scriptura*, the *Book of Concord*, or the Westminster Confession of Faith. These lenses for understanding Christianity came out of Western Christendom, when Christianity was woven into the fabric of Western societies. This was Andrew Walls's point in his lecture in Denmark mentioned in the introduction. Needed for the twenty-first century are concepts and convictions that come out of studying Christian movements through the ages in diverse cultures. As we look at the global movements through the ages, we must be guided by the biblical story and the *global* Christian experience in continuity with its founder. Keep this in mind as we move forward. More to the point, as we will see, Jesus is the key to understanding history, not just Christian history. We will elaborate on this in the next two chapters.

Before deciding on the lens or prior commitments that we will hold onto in our writing and reading of history, it is necessary to ask the preliminary question, Just what is history? We are not asking what is Christian history or what is church history, but what is history itself? History is not what happened, and often it is not what we *think* really happened. *History is a story* that is often confused with what actually happened. We only remember the past as a story, as a narrative. When we do not know all the details, our minds fill in the gaps to give us a story that has cohesion. There is much debate and confusion over the meaning and writing of history, especially the writing of Christian history, so we want to lay out the basic concerns, approaches, and vocabulary before we move on.

WHAT HISTORIANS DO

History is the art of telling, as accurately as possible, *stories* of the past. Thus writing history is not a mere listing of "facts" or evidence nor a tablet on which to etch a particular ideology; still, commitments and beliefs are necessary to the task of telling a meaningful story.

In this section we will look at each of the underscored elements in the above sentence in order. First, we will look at the nature of history as telling a credible story. It involves recreating using one's imagination, but it also involves accuracy, fact-finding, and historical coherence. We all recognize that there is such a thing as bad history or history that does not square with the evidence that is available. Bad history is what keeps historians employed, as we are driven back to research and then suggest ways to correct it.

Second, we will look at the nature of facts or evidence that is available to the historian and what this raw historical material really means for the telling of history. What is regarded as the raw material of history is quite diverse and often does not "prove" what we hope it will prove. The search and selection of historical material depends on the questions we ask. In short, historical research is very complex.

Third, we will turn to various ideologies and philosophies that have guided (and at times repressed) the study of history in the past. In particular we will look briefly at the place of progressivism, positivism, cultural studies, postmodernism, and postcolonial studies. We will comment on how these issues and studies (as distinct from disciplines) have redirected the study of Christianity.

Last, we will look at the place of commitments or beliefs in historical studies. There is a place for belief commitments even in the study of genetics or climate change. In historical studies the debate continues about the proper role, but to deny that there is a place for *belief* is to place one's *faith* in the wrong place.

History as the art of accurate storytelling. Our first point is that history is neither a record of what happened in the past nor a list of supposed facts of the past. History is the art of telling as accurate a story about the past as possible. Because history is the story of people and not things, it is told in a way that reflects how people live and how we hear about human lives.[8] We tell stories because our minds are hard-wired to take in all historical experiences and data as a story. We remember events as part of a stream of related events that carry some sort of meaning. We remember our life as a novel; in fact, a novel is an imitation of our lives as story. Another way of looking at the narrative nature of the human mind is to think about death and grief.

---

[8]In part of a larger argument that leads elsewhere, Bultmann begins his essay on "Christian Faith and History" (1957) asking, "What is the core of history? What is its real subject? The answer is man. . . . The real subject of history is man." Rudolf Bultmann, *History and Eschatology: The Presence of Eternity* (New York: Harper and Row, 1962), 138-39.

Sudden death is like a sudden and unexpected end of a story. Any good counselor or therapist will inform us that grief counseling is very much a matter of letting and even encouraging the grief-stricken to talk about the loved one lost. Telling the story of their life, looking at pictures, and rereading letters and journals—all of these activities help the survivor to make sense of the death and to accept the (possibly) tragic end of a life. Retelling the story of the life helps to complete the story. Life is like that. We are creatures of and for story. History told as raw, unrelated facts is not even history, strictly speaking, because the important detail of causality or connection is missing. There is no history without story. Story connects seemingly unrelated events in cause and effect and gives meaning and purpose to life.

If we need other evidence of the importance of story, we can find it in how we raise children and how religions are communicated. Children's books are all stories, not confessions or dogma. As Dorothy Sayers wisely says, "the dogma is the drama."[9] Even the "children's Bibles" that we find in bookstores are filled with stories. Children learn about the Old Testament and about the life and parables of Jesus when they are young because they love to hear stories. It is very difficult to get a young child to sit down to hear Paul's arguments about the law. Paul's letter to the Romans comes much later in our development. The law apart from the historical narrative is detached and will come across as "inhuman." Children's rhymes and poems are stories—usually short and funny.

Children remember stories, and well-told stories (usually filled with moral lessons) help to guide us into adulthood or continue to irritate us if we choose to ignore their promptings. We enter this world to hear stories, we live our lives as stories, and when we hear about others' lives, we tell stories about them. Even in death, we need to tell and hear stories.

---

[9] Dorothy Sayers, *Creed or Chaos: Why Christians Must Choose Either Dogma or Disaster, or Why It Really Does Matter What You Believe* (London: Hodder and Stoughton, 1939), 5.

The religions of the world also pass on their teachings as myth or story.[10] In most religions the historicity of the myth is not as important as the story itself. When William Carey and his "Serampore Trio" were doing their pioneering mission work in East India, they translated the Hindu epic poem the *Ramayana*. This story of the struggle of good and evil reveals a lot about meaning and how a good Hindu should live in the world. The early missionaries knew that this story would help them and later missionaries to understand the mindset of many in India. Am I saying that this poem is history? No, but I am saying that how the *Ramayana* functions as a meaningful story for those who hear it, tell it, or act it out reveals more about the human need for story. When missionaries arrived in Africa, they would hear the stories of the gods and the ancestors; these stories helped the missionaries more than learning a thousand local aphorisms or laws.

Buddhism also is preserved and presented through story. I remember, right after studying comparative ethics of Theravada Buddhism and Christianity in graduate school, I then made a trip to do some lectures in Thailand. I was full of teachings from the *Jataka Stories*[11] and the *Dhammapada*,[12] and I even had my own copy of the *Dhammapada*. I read these teachings many times and marveled at the similarity of what I considered basic human common sense that is found in so many sacred texts. Then I arrived in Bangkok and took a tour, led by a very culturally astute monk living at a monastery at a new *wat* in the far eastern end of the city. This *wat* had been a major building project; it was the tallest in the city. We toured the grounds and then began our ascent up the inside of the sacred building. Two things struck me. First, as we made the ascent, floor after floor, we saw pictures of the life of Siddhartha Gautama. I recognized most of the

---

[10]We are using the term *myth* here in the general sense of a story with meaning (whether part of history or not).

[11]Stories of the former lives of the Buddha (before he was reincarnated as Siddhartha Gautama).

[12]Proverbial sayings of the Buddha. It reads very much like the book of Proverbs.

scenes as my guide would tell me what was going on in the story, and then he would tell me what the story meant. It was a five-level morality story of how to live by rehearsing the life of Gautama and the experiences of the former lives of the Buddha. My monk-guide explained that most of the people have a hard time meditating on the non-existence of God and self, so the stories of the Buddha help to teach and focus the people on what is true and good. We are made to live and learn from story.

Finally, to underscore my point further, I am reminded of how much students loathe studying history. I have worked to give our guild a better name among undergraduate and graduate students, but in general I still hear, "I can't stand history. All these names and dates. . . . It is just a bunch of meaningless facts." When we hear this response, we are probably hearing students express what history is not supposed to be, or they are expressing their own laziness (you *do* need to learn some facts, even in biology or geometry or geography). A good history class and a good history essay tell a story that is credible, a retelling of a different time and place, that makes sense to the student or the reader. History "means" nothing if it is just a list of things that happened as best as we can reconstruct it. The historian is both scientist and artist, living in constant creative tension in the same body. As we will see later, the historian is also part moral guide.

The stories, told well, stick with us and guide us. M. C. D'Arcy describes how history began: "The past has been kept alive immemorially by word of mouth, by story-telling and ballads and annals."[13] Herbert Butterfield, describing the evolution of history-telling, comments about where history began: "There is ample reason for saying that some things would linger in the memory, at any rate for a time, for the simple reason that the world so loves a good story."[14] These stories, however, mix a good tale with some actual facts, but often the

---

[13]M. C. D'Arcy, *The Sense of History: Secular and Sacred* (London: Faber and Faber, 1959), 18.
[14]Herbert Butterfield, *The Origins of History* (London: Eyre Methuen, 1981), 18.

facts are obscured. The modern historian does not take a good tale as accurate history but sifts through "story telling" along with other historical evidence and then retells a story for today that makes sense of all the evidence. History is always part story. And yet a story can mislead if it is not grounded in facts from the past. But what are these "facts" of the past?

Evidence or facts for the writing of history. Our preoccupation with facts and accuracy in history comes from the Enlightenment. At the same time objective approaches in history writing were developing, Protestant historiography was also developing. A view of history was developed, which persists today, that honors a particular type of knowledge and way of knowing over others that were common in the past.[15] Frankly speaking, it is good to be on this side of the Enlightenment, where ethnic myths, nationalistic stories, and witch hunts are critiqued by carefully recorded history. On the other hand, our scientific approach can miss historical truths that are not recorded as "verifiable facts." The resources of the historian are described as "evidence," and the historian must act as an investigator or a good lawyer studying his or her evidence and then defending its value or exposing its weaknesses. This evidence may come as artwork or shards (for the archaeologist), paintings, diaries, court records, interviews, registries, sermons, or even as older histories. The value of the evidence must be tested against parallel evidence and the accepted scholarship regarding these forms of evidence. After the veracity and the meaning of the many records and materials are received, the story can begin to be told.

The value of good evidence is easily illustrated by the many bad histories that are written in the modern world to support imperialism,

---

[15]Foundational to this approach to church history was the important work of Johann Lorenz von Mosheim (1694–1755), whose four-volume *Institutes of Ecclesiastical History: Ancient and Modern*, ed. H. Soames, trans. J. Murdock (London: Longman, 1841), first published in 1755, was the standard Protestant text for most of the nineteenth century. He claims to have gone to the very sources and given a critical and objective record of church history. See James E. Bradley and Richard A. Muller, *Church History: An Introduction to Research, Reference Works, and Methods* (Grand Rapids, MI: Eerdmans, 1995), 14-16.

nationalism, or racism, or ideologies like Marxism or capitalism.[16] Here the myth of value-free history is exposed. No historian (we should hope) would defend inaccurate history that defends genocide, pogroms, or the use of "comfort women." It is appalling but not surprising that until very recently history books in Japan were written and used that described the role of Japan in early twentieth-century East Asia as beneficent. High school students would read ("factual history") about how Japan helped Korea develop as a nation and how much the Japanese were appreciated as benevolent imperial rulers. China also was depicted as a nation asking for Japan's help, and so Japan came forward as a big brother to help little China. However, the historic facts of ruined lives flatly deny such claims. I have seen photographs of Japanese soldiers crucifying pastors in northern Korea, literally nailing Christians to crosses in mockery because many Christians resisted the imposition of Shinto worship. I have talked to elderly people in Singapore about the treatment of women and pastors. I have been to the Nanjing museum remembering the Nanjing massacre, and I have read journal entries of both businessmen and Christian leaders describing the treatment of prisoners by Japanese soldiers at the Shantung Compound. The evidence—from oral narrative, journals, letters, and pictures—contradicts Japanese nationalist interpretations of the period. This does not mean that the Japanese or the Japanese people are evil (we can find similar moments in the histories of all peoples and religions); it just means that in this case withholding evidence is an injustice and oppression to others. It is bad history, no matter how artistically and beautifully the story is told.

For our historiographic study here, we will also call on evidence, but our evidence will be much more diverse than from traditional histories of Christianity. In building our case for how Christian

---

[16]A recent volume exposes the problem and power of partial histories that have reinforced racism in American Christianity. See Jemar Tisby's *The Color of Compromise: The Truth About the American Church's Complicity in Racism* (Grand Rapids, MI: Zondervan, 2019).

history must be understood today, we will collect and curate evidence from the ancient church in particular because this reveals for us how Christian identity was first developed and perceived in the midst of a sea of paganism and Zoroastrianism (Roman and Parthian Empires). We often talk about the beginning of Christendom with the conversion of Constantine, but it actually took centuries after Constantine before the culture or larger society of the Empire was converted. Thus, Christian writings well past the time of the Council of Nicaea were written in a context of a largely unconverted broader culture. We want to look at these types of writings because there is a closer awareness that Christian teaching and life is peculiar, not culturally normative, but rooted in the paradigmatic life of Jesus. Writings from a later period, say, medieval or Reformation Europe, come from a very different context, one where the struggles are internal and the larger non-Christian world is far away. Second, we will draw on other places in history where Christianity came in contact with other cultures, societies, and religions. This evidence will again highlight Christian identity through contrast and encounter. These encounters come from all the continents (except Antarctica) and include recent encounters, even into the twenty-first century.

Recent philosophies and ideas of history. We live in an age when there is little universal agreement about how history is to be written. I learned this when I presented a paper on the evolution of historiography in the last century to an international group of Christian scholars. I spent a good deal of time talking about postmodernism (Foucault, Lyotard, etc.), which had exhausted me as I tried to understand and then to express it in a coherent three or four pages. I realized that many of the ideas that are tangentially related to postmodern philosophy have become a part of our academic thinking in the West today. When I was done presenting my paper, the Europeans, South Africans, and Australians asked why I spent so much time on postmodern historiography. I was stunned and simply said, "Because it is so important; it is a dominant theme of many of our discussions at the American Academy of Religion and the American Historical Association." I was firmly told that this is just an American thing; Europeans, South Africans, and Australians do not take it that seriously. They may have been overstating their case, but they made their point. Questions of interpretation and methodologies in history are very much in flux, and there is no single or dominant approach today. Still, as an American I am quite aware of the effect of postmodern issues and questions, if not their conclusions, and so here we will look at recent trends in historical studies including postmodern and postcolonial studies.[17] This may be a little tedious, but it is necessary because where we will end up will be in part from an indebtedness to these philosophic movements.

Before World War I, historiography was confident in its scientific clothing. It was an age of progressivism, growing empires, and confidence. It was assumed that history (and the other social sciences) was "scientific," being based on commonly accepted verifiable facts. Such confidence was crushed first during the Great War, and then it suffered a death blow with the rise of Nazism (where "empire" came home to roost). Progressivism had confidence in science and technology, but science and technology also produced mustard gas, firebombing, and atomic weapons. Historicism and positivist history were implicated and thus began a scramble to redefine the parameters and possibilities of history in a way that was scientifically satisfactory.[18] Rather than trying to map all the historiographic approaches that have

---

[17]For a more thorough discussion of these issues, refer to Gertrude Himmelfarb, Keith Jenkins, Donald R. Kelley, Richard Evans, and Georg Iggers, among others. A number of points of departure in the fragmentation of historical study occurred with the French *Annales* school in the 1930s and 1940s with Marc Bloch and Lucien Lebvre, and with the post-critical (and its close cousin postmodern) writings of Derrida, Foucault, and Lacan. Everything began to change in the 1940s and 1950s, at the beginning of the dissolution of empires. See Robin D. G. Kelley's introduction to Aimé Césaire's *Discourse on Colonialism* (New York: Monthly Review, 2000), 7-9.

[18]Gertrude Himmelfarb points out that the "new history" idea goes back to an 1898 article in the *American Historical Review*, but I believe that was a call to a new focus on culture (*Kulturgeshichte*) away from political history, and this did become a central element later. See note 24 below.

blossomed, it will be most helpful for our purposes to identify some of the major themes of and issues with some of the newer "studies."

First, as we have seen above, there has been the debate over just how much history is a science: verifiable, understandable, and repeatable.[19] Can we judge history the way we can judge a chemistry experiment, or the way we can evaluate the results of new experiments on combustion? Historical studies today do not have the same confidence they did in the past, but there are different ways history has been reconstructed. The revisionist movement in history involved rethinking or remaking historical studies, and it has come under many names and brands: "New History," the French *Annales* school, "reconstructionist," deconstructionism, postmodernism, the new historicism, postcolonial or social or cultural history.[20] Each of these reconstructions of history focuses on a new perspective, which often functions as an uncompromising ideology. For our purposes here, it is enough to notice that the positivist confidence in telling a universal history is gone, whether it be a Marxist history or a historicist account.

Key in all of this development was the creative historiographic work that came out of France in the 1920s, but which had a global impact in the writing of history after World War II. The French *Annales* school was less of a philosophy or theory of history than it was a gestalt or new spirit of historical inquiry. The new spirit focused less on institutions and official documents and more on a Durkheimian concern for collective mentalities (at times "collective effervescence")

---

[19]R. G. Collingwood, *The Idea of History*, rev. ed. (New York: Oxford University Press, 1994), 132.
[20]Revisionism was a significant movement in the 1960s, but 1992, the 500th anniversary of the year when "Columbus sailed the ocean blue," was a critical date. All of North American history, and with it Euro-centric, conquest, and "manifest destiny" assumptions, were challenged by authors such as David Stannard (*American Holocaust: Columbus and the Conquest of the New World* [New York: Oxford University Press, 1992]), Kirkpatrick Sale (*The Conquest of Paradise: Christopher Columbus and the Columbian Legacy* [New York: Plume, 1991]), Tzvetan Todorov (*The Conquest of America: The Question of the Other*, trans. Richard Howard [New York: Harper and Row, 1984]), Stephen Greenblatt (*Marvelous Possessions: The Wonder of the New World* [Chicago: University of Chicago Press, 1991]), and Kathy Pelta (*Discovering Christopher Columbus: How History Is Invented* [Minneapolis: Lerner, 1991]).

that helped to explain the history of peoples and cultures.[21] Francesco Chiovaro expresses it well when talking about one of the developments from *Annales*, the new history as history lived by the people:

> I understand, above all, a new mentality of the historians who henceforth regard their discipline open to contributions from other human sciences; to their perspective, to their conclusions, to their methods. Hence the attention drawn particularly to economy, sociology, and geography; then to psychology and to linguistics, and finally to comparative mythology and cultural anthropology.[22]

For the most part this use of social sciences has become common, though not always with an even application of (especially) cultural or anthropological analysis.

Second (and related to this), there have been various debates over the role of the social sciences in the research and writing of history. This is really the biggest story and the one we need to dwell on briefly. Some critiques of the new social science approaches focus on the unmooring of history from traditional history and thus its loss of concern for objectivity, certainty, inductive reasoning, and empirical research.[23] These critics decry the focus on cultural interpretations, linguistics, symbols, hermeneutics, and even multiple rationalities as more than a loss of the "Great Books" curriculum of the past. For the critics, this is a loss of the primary role that history played in the past of searching for and describing truths from the past. History was seen by many as the queen of the social sciences, laying a foundation for other, "softer" sciences that rely on historical research. Previously,

---

[21]See Georg G. Iggers, *Historiography in the Twentieth Century: From Scientific Objectivity to the Postmodern Challenge* (Middleton, CT: Wesleyan University Press, 1997), 51-64.

[22]Francesco Chiovaro, "History as Lived by Christian People: Hypotheses for a New Methodic Approach to Christian History," in *Church History in Ecumenical Perspective*, ed. Lukas Vischer (Bern: Evangelische Arbeitsstelle Oekumene Schweis, 1982), 93.

[23]A sustained argument against "cultural studies" in history is given by Australian historian Keith Windschuttle, *The Killing of History: How Literary Critics and Social Theorists are Murdering Our Past* (San Francisco, CA: Encounter, 1996). His arguments are less about cultural studies than about social theories that function as ideologies, which flatten the complexity of conquest and empire to "good versus evil."

history was written about great people and major events; the history
of nations and of wars were the major subjects. New history focuses
more on the history of the average person as a member of a particular
culture or society.[24] Social context determines the way of thinking
and the use of language. Interpretation of historical events can only
be done by those in that cultural or social context. The use of words
is a political act, giving a person power to interpret self and others.
Therefore, the grand narratives of the past were oppressive political
acts rather than historical descriptions. Gertrude Himmelfarb's en-
gagement with the new history is not neutral, but she does give a
helpful and fair definition of the new emphases:

> Thus, the new history tends to be analytic rather than narrative, thematic
> rather than chronological. It relies more on statistical tables, oral inter-
> views, sociological models and psychoanalytic theories than upon
> constitutions, treaties, parliamentary debates, political writing, or party
> manifestos. Where the old history typically concerns itself with regimes
> and administrations, legislation and politics, diplomacy and foreign
> policy, wars and revolutions, the new history focuses on classes and ethnic
> groups, social problems and institutions, cities and communities, work
> and play, family and sex, birth and death, childhood and old age, crime
> and insanity. . . . The old history is "from above," "elitist history," as is now
> said; the new is "history from below," "Populist history."[25]

She goes on to critique (at length) the new historical methods (plural).
"Where history was once primarily (often entirely) narrative, now it
is primarily (often entirely) analytic."[26] What she means by this is the
tendency for the new historians to lord it over the facts with their
interpretive webs. She, along with Windschuttle, notes that many new
historians deny the integrity of people in the past to act on their own,

---

[24]Gertrude Himmelfarb identified in 1987 that it was not really so new. See the introduction to
The New History and the Old: Critical Essays and Reappraisals, rev. ed. (Cambridge, MA: Harvard
University Press, 2004), 2.

[25]Himmelfarb, *New History and the Old*, 32.

[26]Himmelfarb, *New History and the Old*, 52.

as independent agents, with a multiplicity of causes, robbing the events of their complexity.[27] What Himmilfarb, Windschuttle, and others are reacting to is a tendency toward reductionism by many social historians, psycho-historians, and cultural historians. I think this is a valid critique, as far as it goes.

However, there is a new world of historical research and writing that has opened up thanks to this new focus on the cultural use of language and symbols, the political role of history writing, and turning the focus away from the major figures toward the common people. The *Annales* historians saw their new history as complementary to the history of institutions and "great people," not contradicting what had been done earlier. This earlier historical writing was institutional, tended to be elitist, and focused on the great figures who were not always the best moral exemplars. For Christian history especially, the newer cultural studies guide the historian to ask questions more germane to Christianity:

- Where are the poor?

- How did this ethnic minority understand and witness to their faith?

- How were women involved?

- What language was used?

- How were church conflicts cultural, and how were they theological?

Third, and a subset of the social science approaches above, there is the struggle of other ideologies from within the historical process directing the historical project. Epic events—events larger than life—can become controlling narratives overshadowing the life and identity of a people or a society. The historian can become captive to the event or experience as the grand idea, forcing other narratives and other evidence into the

---

[27]Himmelfarb, *New History and the Old*, 53.

mold of the "great experience." Here we see revealed the nascent power
of the historian as storyteller. One quick example will suffice. When
writing about the history of Serbian Christianity for the second volume
of *History of the World Christian Movement*, I was reading to try to understand the life and spirituality of the Serbian Orthodox Christians of
the seventeenth and eighteenth centuries. Here is what I wrote:

> Damascene of Gabrovo (d. 1771) was a monk in the Serbian Hilander mon-
> astery. After being appointed abbot, he appealed to the Ottoman rulers to
> repay a large debt that they owed the monastery. Through intrigue and de-
> ception, Damascene was falsely accused of having taken a Muslim woman
> into his house, and was given the opportunity to either convert to Islam or
> be hanged. He refused to convert, stating not only his innocence but that he
> was born an Orthodox Christian and would die as such. Rejecting Jesus
> Christ would be the same as rejecting eternal life, he said. Accordingly he
> was hanged, his name entering the ranks of the Serbian saints who resisted.
>
> Theodore Sladich (d. 1788) was another figure from the period who
> opposed Ottoman policies of heavy taxation. He also opposed the spread
> of influences that were coming from western Europe, especially the intro-
> duction of new forms of education that appeared to him to be reducing
> the importance of traditional religious teachings. During Lent of 1788,
> Theodore and 150 of his followers publicly preached against paying the
> heavy taxes to the Turks, linking such resistance to demonstrating one's
> love for God and the saints. For their testimony, all were burned alive. The
> episode demonstrates the degree to which religious and political forms of
> resistance were joined.
>
> *The ethnic identity of Serbs, Bulgarians, and many others continued to*
> *be shaped by what they considered to be oppression, and their resistance to*
> *it.* While most of those involved in the history could not see it at the time,
> in the eighteenth century the Ottoman empire was in a period of slow
> political and economic decline. In the context of this decline, and to a
> degree on account of it, volatile religious divisions gave rise to national-
> istic impulses in the Balkans.[28]

---

[28]Dale Irvin and Scott Sunquist, *History of the World Christian Movement*, vol. 2, *Modern Christianity from 1454 to 1800* (Maryknoll, NY: Orbis, 2012), 2:381-82.

What I put in italics I think can be defended by looking at the writings of the period and by looking at the tradition or history of the Serbs and Bulgarians, even by reading the very recent history of the Balkans. However, it is a dangerous move to shift from saying that this oppression the Serbs suffered has influenced their understanding of themselves and their lives to saying that any history of the Serbs must use these stories (especially the 1389 Battle of Kosovo) as the lens for researching and writing about the Serbs. These periods of suffering are important parts of their history, but to say that they are *the* lens or *the* hermeneutical key is to give them a power like that of an idol. When this happens, history, driven by a particular ideology, shapes people into a particular view of reality or view of themselves. This is an improper use of history, allowing "the idea" to lord over the process or to master the story and the storyteller. I believe that a great deal of our modern ethnic and religious violence and intransigence comes from such historical ideological (or ethnocentric) readings.[29]

Much has been written about other historical approaches that dominate the scene today, but we will only briefly mention them here: postmodern and postcolonial studies. These two approaches or techniques (they are not really cohesive systems or philosophies) have made important contributions to the writing of history. *Postmodern* studies have de-centered historical writing from the hegemony of people like me: North Atlantic white males. When I was studying Asian Christianity in the 1980s, most of what I read was written by missionaries from the West or scholars working with Western records in large libraries in the West. Many of these historians were among the greatest historians of the age. However, they were limited in what they could know and what they could perceive. A Lutheran Batak historian, researching and writing about Christianity and Islam in

---

[29]One small observation here will help keep the argument together. The concept of group identity (ethnic, national, regional, etc.) that I am discussing here comes from Durkheim's concept of "collective" identity, which was heavily used by the French *Annales* historians.

northern Sumatra will see, understand, and write differently about his or her own local history in Batakland. He or she will know the languages, will have in his or her own heart the love and pain of the history. He or she will write a different story.

Many postmodern historians will say that perspective is *everything* and that meaning is *only* in the mind and heart of the local community. Thus, no evaluation or critique can be made of a particular community's interpretation.[30] Expressed in this way it is an extreme position that makes both critique and truth claims impossible. Such an ideology is irresponsible scholarship, and theoretically it prevents intercultural scholarly debate since it gives such prominence to local or cultural interpretations of reality. It also makes international relations nearly impossible. Global understanding as well as peacemaking depend on our ability to understand other cultures and peoples. Postmodern histories can often block the very concern they try to enhance: empathy.

On the other hand, what postmodern historians have given us is insight into the larger story or the deeper understanding of events and people. The value of this contribution to the forgotten cultures and marginalized masses is hard to quantify. This recovery of history we do not want to lose nor belittle. The first task of the historian is to listen to the evidence and listen to other storytellers, noting how they tell their stories. Evaluation and critique must not be lost in the joy of newfound voices that for so long were silenced. Uncritical acceptance of the newer storytellers is paternalistic and unacceptable. However,

---

[30]Windschuttle, *Killing of History*, 279-80, tells the story of Michel Foucault's inventing history to prove his theory. In Foucault's *The Order of Things*, Foucault describes Western taxonomies of animals and compares them with "a certain Chinese encyclopedia," which divides animals according to very different categories (belonging to the emperor; embalmed; tame; sucking pigs). He uses this "history" to illustrate that different cultures have different rationalities. However, the "Chinese encyclopedia Foucault quotes from is fictitious, invented by the Argentine short story writer, Jorge Luis Borges." Historians are often tempted to create history to make a point, but in this case a very radical claim is at stake: different cultures have different rationalities.

historical research with postmodern and social historians as equal dialogue partners is in the best interest of historians of Christianity today. Such intellectual humility will prevent the hermeneutical divide described in the first paragraph of the introduction.

Postcolonial historical writing is closely related to postmodern criticism, recognizing the need for particular cultures and societies that experienced Western colonialism to write their own histories. Postcolonial historians focus on the new context of liberation after colonial oppression. The studies originated as a way of listening to colonized voices that had been silenced for so long. However, in the past few decades the approach has been expanded to include the study of history of all minorities or ethnic groups, whether from former colonies or not. Postcolonial interpretations and approaches are used in most of the social sciences; one can even do a postcolonial analysis of the book of Ruth. Again, we should listen to the basic concern here, recognizing that Christianity started out under an empire (actually both Roman and Parthian). What could be more Christian in historical studies than studying and listening to "the least of these" and the ones who are oppressed by political and religious rulers? However, Christianity was much more than resistance to empire (if it was that at all), so we must also beware of this type of reductionism in historical research and writing.[31]

We want to receive the new approaches of cultural studies without jettisoning the quest for truth, inductively researched and received. We want to understand the life and history of a particular indigene on their own terms without saying that their particular language and culture of interpretation is something that we cannot understand. We want to encourage cultural history but not let it become an ideology that makes *multicultural* history-telling impossible: we can talk about

---

[31]For a critique of this view of first and second century Christianity as resistance to empire, see Scott Sunquist, "Hidden History," *The Christian Century*, September 18, 2006, https://www.christiancentury.org/reviews/2006-09/hidden-history.

and be challenged by others even though they are from another culture.[32] Thus, in our twenty-first-century global culture, we must affirm both the particular local interpretations *and* the need for global connectiveness. Our appreciation for local cultures and societies must not prevent us from our search for common understandings of peace and justice. Cultural studies can unwittingly support new forms of tribalism and division. History is foundational for other social sciences, and therefore it must not abandon its role as truth-teller, cross-culturally or even globally received. It must not sacrifice the unity and peace of humankind on the altar of a de facto cultural absoluteness.

Faith commitments and Christian history. Finally, it is important to recognize that all historians have beliefs about the world, the cosmos, God/gods, spirits, and the dead/ancestors. These beliefs will influence what is researched and how the story is told. We have mentioned the three voices or threads that should help to guide our history writing: Scripture, the global church, and continuity with the life of Jesus. A person can be guided by these and still not have Christian faith. In other words, a person can believe that Christianity should be critiqued on its own terms but not be a believer herself.

What we are saying here is that historians should be clear about what philosophy or ideology is framing their narrative, but they should also state clearly that they are telling a story that they are part of or that they are discovering and talking about people who are not in their own community of faith. Does this matter? I think it does. Let me explain.

In telling stories where Christians describe something unnatural or supernatural (miraculous), we might just drop the story completely if we do not believe such things happen. Or we might simply say,

---

[32]These convictions of the value of local histories and the need for global scholarship were foundational for two scholarly community projects that have shaped my scholarship: *A Dictionary of Asian Christianity* (1991–2001, involving over 480 scholars) and *History of the World Christian Movement* (1998–2010, involving about fifty scholars).

"Some of the local Christians reported that . . ." Or we might find it a quite credible story given the three voices to which we are listening and by which we are guided. The person telling a story from the inside, as it were, will be more attentive to issues like the specific words about Jesus' identity, the meaning of the Trinity, or the role, function, and power of the sacraments. This will be a major theme in chapter three on the cross.

We turn now from historical writing in general to the Christian story, or what is generally called church history. In this turn we are now looking at how to engage in the study of Christian history with the newer, more interdisciplinary study of historical periods. As a reminder, what has made it necessary to rethink how we approach the history of Christianity is the transformation that took place in the late twentieth century. Our basic assumptions about Christianity and its development have been challenged and, in fact, have proven to be inadequate. So, now it is time to look at the first of three threads that make up the cord of Christian history: an understanding of time itself.

Chapter Two

Time: Creation and Incarnation

*I can't understand why you missionaries present the Bible to us
in India as a book of religion. It is not a book of religion—and anyway
we have plenty of books of religion in India. We don't need any more!
I find in your Bible a unique interpretation of universal history,
the history of the whole of creation and the history of the human race.
And therefore a unique interpretation of the human person as
a responsible actor in history. That is unique. There is nothing else
in the whole religious literature of the world to put alongside it.*

LESSLIE NEWBIGIN

*For the Christian view of history is not merely a belief in the direction
of history by divine providence, it is a belief in the intervention of God
in the life of mankind by direct action at certain definite points in time
and place. The doctrine of the Incarnation which is the central doctrine
of the Christian faith is also the centre of history, and thus it is appropriate
that our traditional Christian history is framed in a chronological system
which takes the year of the incarnation as its point of reference
and reckons its annals backwards and forwards from this fixed center.*

CHRISTOPHER DAWSON

Long ago God spoke to our ancestors in many and various ways
by the prophets, but in these last days he has spoken to us by a Son,
whom he appointed heir of all things, through whom he also created
the worlds. He is the reflection of God's glory and the exact imprint
of God's very being, and he sustains all things by his powerful word.
When he had made purification for sins, he sat down
at the right hand of the Majesty on high.

HEBREWS 1:1-3

BACK IN THE TWENTIETH CENTURY when I studied church history, I was taught using books that had the following characteristics: they were mostly doctrinal history, focused on great leaders (mostly white males), were apologies for Protestantism, and covered mostly Western Christianity. Identity is created by one's history or what is told about one's past. Memory is identity. Such a history as I was taught predisposed me to understand Christianity in a particularly limited way. Both the development of a more interdisciplinary historiography and the development of Christianity as a worldwide movement requires us to research and write differently. This much should be clear. However, the diverse approaches which we have just been looking at may seem to obscure our way forward.

In fact it may seem best just to return to a "scientific" approach to the research and writing of history. Can't we write history as "just the facts"? Is it possible to avoid the overarching ideologies we have looked at that massage and shape historical evidence into our own image? No to the first question, because history is always a story that selects what "facts" to tell and how to connect them. Yes to the second question, for it is possible to tell a faithful narrative that is both a human story and God's story. That is what this book is about.

The faith commitments and perspective of the historian are necessary, but it is a matter of whether those faith commitments are better or worse than earlier Enlightenment approaches, globally considered. It is our thesis here that the faith commitments that are necessary to understand and study Christian history *on its own terms* are an understanding of *time, cross,* and *glory.* The Christian concept of time (and incarnation), the central role of the cross (and suffering), and the Christian preoccupation with the revelation of the glory of God must guide our studies of Christianity. These are specifically Christian commitments and perspectives that make the telling of the Christian story reasonable, coherent, and lucid. We begin here with the first of these three threads, for as Arnold Toynbee said so clearly, "Christianity [is] the historical religion par excellence."[1]

TIME AND INCARNATION: HISTORY IS BORN

Time is both meaningful and purposeful for the Christian. But what is that purpose and meaning? It should be clear to us now that the positivist and colonial histories represented by books like *Christian Missions and Social Progress* are a far cry from the new social histories of the late twentieth and early twenty-first centuries. History writing, including the questions being asked and the subjects of concern, has had a great transformation in the last century. As we turn now from history writing in general to the writing of Christian history, we can see, even in the pictures from Dennis's book and in his attitude of progress for all nations, that the Christian idea of time and hope was deeply embedded in his theology. In fact, for all our criticisms of nineteenth-century progressivism, social gospel optimism, or Student

---

[1]Arnold Toynbee, "The Christian Understanding of History," in *God, History and the Historians,* ed. C. T. McIntire (New York: Oxford University Press, 1977), 182.

Volunteer triumphalism,[2] we can see that the hope of the gospel is expressed in all of these.

Another way this can be expressed is as follows: *something was done in the past that has a present reality and gives a future hope.* It is my argument that this is a universal quality of Christianity, whether the hope comes from, to, or in spite of colonial powers. Hope is central to Christianity in part because there is a belief in time: time is not merely the recapitulation of the past but moves forward toward a goal. In Jesus Christ, hope is offered. The incarnation is the event in time that initiates a new understanding of time from creation to the new creation. The incarnation event (and what follows) is described as forgiveness, liberation, healing, salvation, and redemption. It comes in many forms. However, in Jesus Christ there is a future that includes a purpose and goal. History as an ongoing and purposeful story is important. Why do we make such a big issue of time? In part because it is a big issue, but also because it is not universally true for all cultures and religions. Christianity invented time as we commonly understand it today.

Let's put this in historical context. One of the great tragedies of the modern and now postmodern era is the disdain we have developed for history, and especially for religious history and tradition. In a sense we have ourselves to blame for this since the anti-historical bias that developed in the Enlightenment was very much a result of the betrayal of religion by Western societies. Religion, which is supposed to give solace, comfort, meaning, and "healing for the nations" had become the crusader against the East and the inquisitor in the West. As Descartes looked over the seventeenth-century battlefields where Christians were killing other Christians over political power and interpretations of the Eucharist, he felt that all knowledge was misleading. And here is the rub: Descartes reasoned that what we

---

[2] "The evangelization of the world in this generation" was the watchword of the SVM.

had known through history and tradition misled us, so we need to start afresh. What we were told from history cannot be trusted, so I have to begin with myself: *cogito ergo sum*. I can trust myself, reasoned Descartes.

Two revolutions occurred at the same time, and we still live with these two today. The first revolution was a turn away from history and a turn toward the future. This meant a turn away from tradition or the past as bearer of truth and an anchor for the present. Truth was no longer found in the past but in what was modern and what was to come. The future, and human progress that brings us there, holds truth. The West became known for its devotion to all things new, and thus it devoted its best talents to building a future. The second turn was a turn away from God and God's church to the "self" as the measure of truth. The scientific method developed, even among well-meaning Christians, at a time when history was on the decline. The Reformation cry of "*ad fontes*" ("to the sources") turned into the Enlightenment cry of Kant, "*Sapere aude!*" ("Dare to know!"). And knowing involved daring to discover and think something new. In fact, two of the proofs of truth in the "modern" world are "Is it new?" and "Does it work?" Pragmatism and innovation reign supreme. So we live with this modern epistemological heresy, where history contains no knowledge and certainly no wisdom. In earlier times history had meaning. Post-Enlightenment humans must create their own meaning and identity.

Time Is Central, and It Has a Center

History, or more exactly the Christian view of history, is the exact opposite. It is neither irrelevant nor boring. In fact, history is meaningful because it has a beginning, a center, and a culmination. They are all connected, and they make sense only if all three are woven together in a shared story. The center, the incarnation, is understood as the pivotal event in all of history. God enters the created realm and in doing so lifts up the creation. What was distant and separated from God has now become God's own flesh or tabernacle. In God's coming down and "putting on," we have been "lifted up." A sacred time and a sacred space, in a particular cultural context, sacralized what was tarnished and lost in despair. The incarnation is the turning point in history. This is not a recurring happening, nor is it an imagined myth; it is a singular event in history with timeless consequences.

With the coming of Christ as the sent one of God came a new view of reality, one that confronted the cyclical views of reality that were common in the Roman Empire as well as among many of the religions of the world at that time. The coming of the Savior was foretold as a hope for Israel. However, the reality was both much more cosmic and at the same time much more humble. As Christians told that story to Hellenists in the West and Zoroastrians in the East, it was clear that it challenged basic understandings about life, time, and death.

We often fail, in our zeal for what is new, to realize the radical nature of Christianity when it came on the scene. Patristic scholars and historians of the ancient Near East are familiar with the worldview shift that took place with the advent of Christianity, but most historians who focus their attention on the early period have lost the significance because they are so often writing within and about Christendom. Christendom assumes the Christian understanding of time so thoroughly that to ask a Christendom historian about the radical nature of time that came with the advent of Christianity is like asking a fish about water. What were the general assumptions about time that were prevalent in the ancient Near East, and how was Christianity a radical departure from this?

There was no single view of time and history in the first century world that cradled the early church, but there were some common themes. In general it must be remembered that most nature religions or hierophanic faiths come out of and live close to nature and nature's cycles. Thus, "time" had a certain sacredness, but its sacredness comes with the seasons: a new moon festival, or a festival of harvest, planting, or vernal equinox. Most all people were illiterate farmers or herdsmen in the ancient world, so they were guided by the stars, the moon, and the sun. In tropical regions they were guided by cycles of rain and drought. With such a view of the holy or sacred, people develop a cyclical view of time. History, or the cycles of time, tends to be attached to the stories of the fathers and mothers and remembering the ancestors. Again, this can and often does reinforce a cyclical view of time, since the ancestors, like us, lived and died.

The Greeks are said to have invented the modern concept of time, but for the most part Greeks were philosophers—discussing how to live now—rather than historians.[3] Herodotus and Thucydides were the first to lay down what would become standard "scientific" procedures of testing sources and historical investigation. However, the Greeks had a short view of history with little interest in those who came before them. In fact, the Greeks had accepted a variation of "cyclical history," a periodic view that taught that there are recurrent catastrophes that completely destroy civilization. Cultures must periodically start over again. This is a type of cyclical view of history, but it is not the cyclical view of the Indians nor of most Bedouins. Herbert Butterfield summarizes the Greek view of history neatly:

> They may have had almost an inkling of the idea of progress, for they soon arrived at the view that mankind has to rise from a primitive stage, gradually learning the various arts and sciences. What really held them up was their theory of catastrophe, bringing the human race perpetually back to the beginning again. Time, as they thought they experienced it, was cyclic therefore, and utterly pointless to them.

Butterfield then goes on to prove his point quoting Plato and Polybius. Plato believed that a god sets the world in motion in one direction

---

[3]For a full discussion of Greek views of history, especially in contrast to Egyptian and Christian views, see Herbert Butterfield, *Origins of History*, chaps. 4 and 6. The following paragraph is taken from Butterfield's excellent summary.

and then withdraws his hand. The world reverses, so everything turns bad until he returns to set things back in the correct direction. Polybius, less than two centuries before Christ, taught a periodic destruction of most of the human race. He even said, "Reason tells us [this] may often happen again, all the traditions and arts will simultaneously perish . . . [and then later a] renewal of social life will begin."[4]

Georges Florovsky describes the classical mind regarding history as fatalistic and pessimistic.

> History was a story of unavoidable doom and decay. Men were confronted with a dilemma. On the one hand they could simply "resign" and reconcile themselves to the inevitability of "destiny." . . . Or on the other hand, men could attempt an escape, a "flight" out of history, out of this dimension of flux and change—the hopeless wheel of genesis and decay—into the dimension of the changeless. . . . Consequently, there was no room for any pro-gress, but only for "re-volutions," recirculation, cyclophoria and anacyclosis. . . . Accordingly, there was no reason and no motive, to look forward, into the future.[5]

The universe functioned according to rules, and time was a matter of set rhythms, not of movement in any direction. "Nor was the uniqueness of any event acknowledged. Only 'patterns' were relevant."[6] Into this world of reigning assumptions came an event which claimed to be unique and looked forward to a completion or fulfillment of what had been started.

The Jesus event is described throughout the New Testament as epoch-making or as a defining historic occurrence not limited to a small plot of Middle Eastern soil. Matthew indicates that even the spirits or demons recognize the significance of Jesus Christ. When Jesus crossed the sea and stepped onto predominantly Gentile

[4]Butterfield, *Origins of History*, 125.

[5]From Florovsky's essay, "The Predicament of the Christian Historian," in *God, History, and the Historians: An Anthology of Modern Christian Views of History*, ed. C. T. McIntire (New York: Oxford University Press, 1977), 431-32.

[6]Florovsky, "Predicament of the Christian Historian," 431-32.

territory, two demons shouted at him, "What have you to do with us, Son of God? Have you come here to torment us before the time?" Jesus talks about "harvest time" (Mt 21:34, 41), "on that day" (Mt 7:22), and at the "proper time" (Mt 24:45). And of course there was a sense that he was marked for a particular event at a particular time: "My time is near; I will keep this Passover at your house with my disciples" (Mt 26:18). In Mark, Jesus' first words indicate that time is of the essence, or is essential: "The time is fulfilled, and the kingdom of God has come near; repent, and believe in the good news" (Mk 1:15). In the famous inaugural passage of Jesus' ministry as recorded in Luke, Jesus reads about liberation, the time of jubilee, and then, when everyone is sitting in rapt attention, he says, "Today this scripture has been fulfilled in your hearing" (Lk 4:21). Jesus announced the advent of an important time, and he criticized the people for being fickle and not being able to read the times. "You hypocrites! You know how to interpret the appearance of earth and sky, but why do you not know how to interpret the present time?" (Lk 12:56). Others seemed clueless about the "time," but Jesus was clear about interpreting the time: he was actually himself the interpretive key for all of time.

When performing the first recorded miracle in Cana of Galilee, his mother tells Jesus that they are out of wine, and his cryptic response is simply, "Woman, what concern is that to you and to me? My hour has not yet come" (Jn 2:4). The Gospel authors were clear that Jesus' life was significant for time:

1. He was the fulfillment of prophecies.

2. He foretold his own suffering and death.

3. He foretold a future of both judgment and hope.

4. His authority over spirits and creation marked a new age.

Without going through all of the New Testament regarding the issue of time, we can simply state what all the Christians realized: Jesus ushered in a new age and a new movement. This theme is so strong that some have seen it as the primary identity of Jesus Christ: an eschatological prophet.[7] We might say that for the earliest Christians the whole new world that was initiated meant that history was God's idea.[8] The cycle of birth, growth, decay, death, and rebirth was broken when God came to usher in a new kingdom on earth that pointed to a fulfillment time in the future. Time was torn asunder from the endless and hopeless wheel of futility and given direction and hope.

As the early Christians began to reflect on this event, they rightly discovered that the origin of salvation was actually found in creation. Creation became a central, or at least foundational, salvific event. How did this happen? How did a contemporary event so quickly become linked with creation? Very simply, the doctrine of redemption led them back to creation; the redeemer led them back to the Creator. Athanasius, for example, begins his discussion of "On the Incarnation of the Word of God" (*De incarnatione verbi dei*) by talking about creation. The one who created humanity is the only one to redeem humanity. Only the one who created humanity, the one who understands the "original design," can bring humanity back or redeem (buy humanity back). This helps to explain why there are so many patristic commentaries and homilies on Genesis, and more specifically on the *Hexaemeron* (the six days of creation). Ephrem, John Chrysostom, Diodore of Tarsus, Basil, Narsai, Origen, Ambrose, Augustine, and Cyril of Alexandria all wrote commentaries on the first six days of creation.[9] The early defenders of the faith would agree with Martin Luther: "*Nihil pulchrius Genesi, nihil utilius*" ("Nothing more beautiful than Genesis, nothing more useful").[10] This new understanding

---

[7]See Dale Allison, *Jesus of Nazareth: Millenarian Prophet* (Minneapolis: Augsburg, 1998).

[8]Andrew Louth, *Maximus the Confessor* (London: Routledge, 1996), 63-77; John Behr, *The Mystery of Christ: Life in Death* (Crestwood, NY: St. Vladimir's Seminary Press, 2006).

[9]See Fr. Seraphim Rose, *Genesis, Creation, and Early Man: The Orthodox Christian Vision* (Platina: St. Herman, 2000).

[10]James Strahan, *Hebrew Ideals: A Study of Genesis 11–50*, 4th ed. (Edinburgh: T&T Clark, 1922), 5.

of reality, where God created all things, including time, was a radical break with the common understanding of the ancient world.[11]

CREATIO EX NIHILO

Closely connected to the creation of time was the new concept of *creatio ex nihilo* ("creation out of nothing"). God did not fashion out of pre-existent stuff; he created the stuff. Ancient Christian writers wrote about creation to show that God's redemption is in fact a creation and creative work that God alone has done. Most pagan myths of creation are pessimistic about creation. Creation is a corruption, a mistake, or a pollution. Humanity is not a glorious crown of creation; in most myths, the physical universe, including the human body, is an error or even an evil to be conquered or released from. In stark contrast, creation as taught by the early apostles was intentional, purposeful, and glorious. It was not something to escape but something to be sanctified. Thus creation was not derivative, a corruption from something else, but it had its own origin and integrity in the mind of God.

We can see how important it was to understand God's absolute creation out of nothing when we look at the response of patristic authors to Origen. Origen's theology of creation was seen as semi-Platonic, so his views were criticized, and his works on creation were not included in the *Philokalia*.[12] Creation out of nothing was a radical departure from the Greek view of the world, a world where intermediaries moved between the realm of ideas and the physical plane.

---

[11]This new understanding of time was just as epoch-making in Zoroastrian Persia as in the European and African world. Zoroastrians believed there were dual creators, one creating good (Ahura Mazda) and one creating evil (Ahriman). See Scott Sunquist, "Narsai and the Persians" (PhD diss., Princeton Theological Seminary, 1990).

[12]Origen's view of creation and time has recently been re-evaluated, but the historic fact is that Origen's interpretation of the Bible was appreciated by Orthodoxy and is included in the *Philokalia,* but his views on creation were left out. The Cappadocian Basil of Caesarea explicitly rejected his interpretation of Genesis, his views seeming a little too Platonic. Origen's disembodied eschatology or idealism does not provide adequate basis for social activity on behalf of justice, nor does it promote the cultural mandate (Gen 1:26-28, to fill the earth, subdue it, and have dominion), which has been a central pillar of Christian history.

Some in the ancient church had a very difficult time accepting such an extreme doctrine—not only Origen but also various Gnostic theologies compromise on creation *ex nihilo.*

The centrality of this doctrine, not only for the early church but throughout Christian history, can be seen in how the doctrine is expressed in the *Philokalia.*[13] Why do we look at this compiled work? Because the *Philokalia* is a good indicator of both the development of an idea over time (from the fourth through the tenth centuries), and it is a type of gold standard of theology for the Eastern Church. And in this gold standard, the largest sections are devoted to Maximus the Confessor (580–662), which exceeds two hundred pages. The works are deeply theological and practical, concerned with right thinking about God, which will nurture a life of Christian virtues. In a number of places in his *Four Hundred Sayings on Love* Maximus talks about creation, God as the creator, and the proper contemplation of creation. Improper contemplation leads to vices, and so there is a clear connection between right thinking about creation and righteousness for Maximus.

> All immortal things and immortality itself, all living things and life itself, all holy things and holiness itself, all good things and goodness itself, all blessings and blessedness itself, all beings and being itself are manifestly works of God. Some things began to be in time, for they have not always existed. Others did not begin to be in time, for goodness, blessedness, holiness, and immortality have always existed. Those things which began in time exist and are said to exist by participation in the things which did not begin in time. For God is the creator of all life, immortality, holiness and goodness; and He transcends the being of all intelligible and describable beings.[14]

---

[13] A collection of the most valuable writings from the Eastern (Orthodox) Church during the first millennium. These writings were collected in 1782 and made available to the English-speaking world about 1979. St. Nikodimos of the Holy Mountain and St. Makarios of Corinth, *The Philokalia*, trans. Kallistos Ware, G. E. H. Palmer, and Philip Sherrard, 4 vols. (London: Faber and Faber, 1979–1995).

[14] "Two Hundred Texts on Theology and the Incarnate Dispensation of the Son of God," in *Philokalia*, 2:124.

Only God and his character (holiness, etc.) have existed from before time. What has been created is dependent on or participates in what is eternal. "God has brought things into existence out of nothing. . . . Some say that the created order has coexisted with God from eternity; but this is impossible. . . . This notion is drawn from the pagan Greek philosophers, who claim that God is in no way the creator of being but only of qualities. . . . Created things have not coexisted with God from eternity."[15] He goes on extensively discussing creation and the absolute distance between God and God's creation out of nothing. We could go on about Maximus and others, but the point is clear: only a doctrine of God creating, as opposed to fashioning or shaping, is the proper foundation for Christian thought and life.

The implication of this radical claim has been spelled out by Andrew Louth. He notes that "both Athanasius and Arius have a very clearly defined doctrine of creation *ex nihilo*. This may not seem very surprising until it is realized that the doctrine was unknown to pagan philosophy and only emerged slowly and uncertainly in early Christian theology. . . . With Athanasius and Arius, there is no doubt, for they enumerate the alternatives and reject them." What this means, says Louth, is that there is a complete contrast between God and his creation, or between the divine (uncreated) and that "which is created out of nothing but the will of God."[16] Therefore, there is no intermediate zone; there are no aeons or emanations. It was this intermediate world (posited by Middle Platonism, e.g., Philo) that contained the idea of Logos, but since the Christian view of creation had no middle zone, the Logos had to be identified fully with God (Athanasius and the Orthodox) or fully with the world (Arius).

---

[15]"Two Hundred Texts on Theology and the Incarnate Dispensation of the Son of God," in *Philokalia*, 2:100.

[16]Andrew Louth, *The Origins of the Christian Mystical Tradition: From Plato to Denys*, 2nd ed. (Oxford: Oxford University Press, 2007), 73.

The soul, it was soon understood—in contradistinction to Origen—also was created *ex nihilo*; it is part of creation. Thus Christian mystical theology *does not see the soul as part of God.* For Athanasius the soul is a mirror of God. Louth comments, "There is no ontological continuity between the image of the mirror and of that which it is the image; so, in the case of the soul reflecting the image of God, this similarity discloses a much deeper dissimilarity at the level of substance."[17] For Athanasius the soul is created; it is not part of God. The soul is something new and different but reflecting something much greater: the image of God. The soul is greatly valued as reflecting the triune God, but the soul is not God.

CREATION THAT IS THOROUGHLY GOOD

Creation of all things, seen and unseen, is out of nothing, and this creation is also good—not just fairly good, or good in part, but thoroughly and completely good in each of its parts and in its cosmic whole. Partially and completely, God's creation out of nothing is "very good" (Gen 1:31). Jewish and Christian teaching that the physical creation is good is also a key component to our understanding of time. Many if not most religions and cultures of this world look at the suffering and natural disasters of the world and conclude that the physical world is inferior to a purely spiritual existence. Creation, as described in Genesis, is fascinating to most non-Christian people of the world. These descriptions of creation are beautiful stories of a bountiful, harmonious creation of mutuality and peace. A good, diverse, and beautiful creation serves God's image (humanity) that is over all of the created order. Again, most non-Christian creation accounts are not so "good"; they are filled with the failure, corruption, or evil of the physical world from the beginning.

---

[17]Louth, *Origins of the Christian Mystical Tradition*, 77.

What this means in our view of time is that the creation that we see (earth) as well as don't see (heavens) is good, and it is to be embraced.[18] It is not that the souls of people are good but the bodies are bad. No! There is no dichotomy in this goodness created by God. It is the embodied life of humans who are created to support or care for the immensely diverse creation, which is very good. Even with its prickliness and unpredictable times and places of suffering, creation—including human life—is good and meaning-full. Life, beginning with family ("it is not good that the man should be alone," Gen 2:18) and work ("fill the earth and subdue it," Gen 1:28) is not to be escaped from but lived into.

And yet we suffer. Suffering is an issue in all religions, and most religions find their genesis in trying to make sense of suffering and death. Evil, usually as a personal being, is part of this explanation for suffering and death. Answers to these questions vary, but they are based on assumptions about time, creation, good, and evil. Christianity is unique in its positive view of creation as being rooted in the will of a good and loving Creator God.

Below we look at different views of creation that, in contrast to the Christian view we have just looked at, show a resistance to the robust view of a *good* creation made *ex nihilo* by a good God.

CHRISTIAN SCIENCE

Christian Science was organized in 1866 by Mary Baker Eddy (1821–1910). Baker Eddy was brought up in a strict Congregationalist family in New Hampshire. From childhood she suffered from chronic illness and was prone to depression, but in 1866 after suffering a serious back injury from a fall, Baker Eddy experienced healing that she claimed came about from reading the Gospel of Matthew. This launched her

---

[18]"In the beginning . . . God created the heavens and the earth," meaning the seen and unseen (Gen 1:1). Earth and heaven are mentioned three times in the first two chapters. Colossians 1:16 exegetes this using the parallelism "for in Him [Jesus] all things in heaven and on earth were created, things visible and invisible [or seen and unseen]." This is repeated in referring to the work of redemption in Col 1:20: "all things, whether on earth or in heaven."

on a theological journey that culminated in the publication in 1875 of *Science and Health*. According to Baker Eddy, all reality is ultimately spiritual in nature. She starts with an uncompromising dualism between matter and spirit. The material world is without enduring substance, unlike the divine, which is eternal. Humanity is not material in essence but spiritual. Christ is truly divine but became material for a time to teach humanity the divine science, the path to salvation. This is why studying the teachings of Christ as found in the Bible can lead to salvation. Even his death was essentially didactic. Jesus submitted to death in order to be resurrected in his eternal, spiritual form, demonstrating to his followers the non-reality of the material world. Since God can only create what is good, sin has no reality, and disease and death (which are part of physical bodies) are caused by illusion. Prayer brings one into harmony with God and thereby overcomes sin, sickness, and disease.

Christian Science affirms in their weekly worship, "There is no life, truth, intelligence, nor substance in matter. All is infinite Mind and its infinite manifestation, for God is All-in-all. Spirit is immortal Truth; matter is mortal error. Spirit is the real and eternal; matter is the unreal and temporal."[19]

UNITY SCHOOL OF CHRISTIANITY

Closely related to Christian Science is Unity, also known as Unity Church. Unity is a religious movement within the wider New Thought movement and is best known to many through its Daily Word devotional publication. Its founder, like Mary Baker Eddy, suffered illness as a child and came to similar conclusions about the world. Myrtle Fillmore (1845–1931) was raised in a Methodist household in Ohio. As a child she contracted tuberculosis but was able to complete a year

---

[19]From the "Scientific Statement of Being," which is to be read at each Christian Science worship service. This is found in the chapter "Recapitulation," in Mary Baker Eddy, *Science and Health with Key to the Scriptures* (Boston: Christian Science Publishing Society, 1917), 468.

of study at Oberlin College and take a position as a teacher. In 1881 she married Charles Fillmore (1854–1948), whom she met in Denison, Texas, while undergoing treatment for her tuberculosis. The two moved to Kansas City, where in 1886 they began attending lectures by a proponent of what was called "metaphysical teaching," or "New Thought." New Thought teachers, similar to Mary Baker Eddy, held that physical illness had spiritual causes and that the basis for physical healing was found in the mental world. Myrtle Fillmore was cured of her tuberculosis. She and Charles began systematizing their ideas and organizing prayer groups for healing that they called "Silent Unity." In 1889 they began devoting their efforts full time to the prayer groups, and around 1895 they began to call their movement simply "Unity," or the "Unity School of Christianity." For the Fillmores, God is the underlying positive principal of love that animates all things in the universe. Christ is that spirit of love that lives inside each human being. Affirmative prayer releases negative thoughts and connects one to the divine, bringing about healing in both body and soul, or the physical and the spiritual dimensions. The goal is closer to Hinduism than Christianity: after a number of reincarnations, the soul, released from the body, attains perfect oneness with God.

GNOSTICISM

Gnostic views of creation are diverse but share a common denigration of the physical world.[20] Although we don't see many Gnostic churches today, the influence of Gnostic predispositions continues in many forms of Christianity up to the present. The Gnostics found Christian teachings too simple and *koine* (common). In fact Gnosticism tends to be for the well-educated and the elite. Gnostic teaching assumes that behind creation there is an earlier story and a more complex

---

[20]For a more thorough introduction to Gnostic themes see Dale T. Irvin and Scott W. Sunquist, *History of the World Christian Movement*, vol. 1, *Earliest Christianity to 1453* (Maryknoll, NY: Orbis Books, 2001).

cosmology that includes other deities, spirits, and *aeons*. These are secret teachings that Jesus only told to some secretly.

Two of the great Gnostic teachers reflect the two basic types of Gnosticism. Both taught from Rome. Valentinus (c. 100–c. 160), originally from Alexandria, came to Rome in about AD 140 and gathered many followers around him with his creative teaching.

> Without a doubt he was among the greatest Gnostic minds, skillfully blending his own speculative insights with biblical stories and Platonic philosophical doctrine to create a comprehensive system of salvation. Valentinus taught that God is a threefold mystery from whom emanates some thirty orders of Aeons of heavenly worlds. These Aeons represented attributes in male and female form. The last of them included the Mother figure, Sophia ("Wisdom").[21]

At some point Sophia's extreme desire to fathom the Forefather led to her disrupting the Pleroma ("Fullness"), and this led to the birth of a demiurge, or lesser god, which created the physical universe and humanity. There is much more to this story and other stories, but the point to be made here is that creation is a mistake born out of impatience and desire. What is physical is a departure from what is good.

The second type of Gnosticism is that of Marcion (c. 85–c. 160), who came from a wealthy family in Pontus (Turkey) and traveled to Rome to join the church and provide teaching about Jesus. His teaching was radically dualistic, positing that the God of the Old Testament (YHWH) was the demiurge who created the physical universe, and he himself was limited and had a physical body. The God of Jesus was all love and compassion; the God of the Old Testament was a God who punished and judged. Jesus was all spirit who appeared to have been in the flesh, but he was not actually. What is physical is evil, so Jesus could not have a body.

---

[21]Irvin and Sunquist, *History of the World Christian Movement* 1:116.

These and many other Gnostic teachings depart from the Christian view of creation and time in the following ways:

1. The physical world is bad, fallen or a mistake. Creation is like a prison.

2. Women are undervalued (in most systems they must become a men through rebirth before they can be saved).

3. Gnostics are elitist and secret. Jesus' teachings were for the poor and were public.

4. The goal is release from suffering and the physical body.

5. Intermediary divine *aeons* preexist the creator God.

6. Gnosticism is docetic (Jesus only appeared to be human). Thus, the cross is not a victory but a tragedy.[22]

7. Gnosticism generally led to antinomianism because of the dichotomy of flesh and spirit.

In an early sermon that has been called "Clement's Second Letter to the Corinthians," we see how important the Christian doctrine of a good creation is for our salvation. "Moreover, let none of you say that this flesh will not be judged or rise again. . . . We should guard the flesh as God's temple. For just as you were called in the flesh, you will come in the flesh. If Christ the Lord who saved us was made flesh though he was at first spirit, and called us in this way, in the same way we too in this very flesh will receive our reward."[23]

HINDUISM, BUDDHISM, AND TRANSMIGRATION OF SOULS

Both Hinduism and its reform movement, Buddhism, assume that time is cyclical and that souls transmigrate in cycles of birth, life, suffering, death, and rebirth. Creation itself, or stories of "beginnings,"

---

[22]See Donald Fairbairn, *Life in the Trinity: An Introduction to Theology with the Help of the Church Fathers* (Downers Grove, IL: IVP Academic, 2009), 169-71.

[23]From Cyril C. Richardson, ed., *Early Christian Fathers* (New York: Macmillan, 1970), 196.

are not uniform and express many speculations. One of the most important of Hindu texts, the *Rigveda*, is agnostic regarding creation. *Rigveda* 10 expresses it well:

> Who really knows? Who will here proclaim it?
> Whence was it produced? Whence is this creation?
> Gods came afterwards, with the creation of this universe.
> Who then knows whence it has arisen?[24]

However, the goal of life is to escape this created world of suffering and endless cycles of birth and rebirth (samsara), thus denigrating created existence. In Buddhism, *Nirvana* (Sanskrit) or *Nibbana* (Pali) is the spiritual goal of the believer. Etymologically Nirvana means to be "snuffed out" or "quenched." What this means is an end to the re-births of samsara. Although there are various interpretations within Buddhism of what this existence or non-existence might be, there is no disagreement that it means release from this physical world of suffering caused by attachment. It is a release to non-existence or stillness.

SECULAR EVOLUTION

Many Christians today adhere to moderated or limited views of evolution that see God's creative hand behind natural and social developments and in nature at large. These views of theistic evolution uphold God as the creator of all, who set time in motion through this creation. What we are talking about here, however, is a *secular* evolution that posits that somehow energy exploded in a big bang, setting in motion the very long cooling process that eventually made life possible. Most secular views of evolution place little value on the universe or think it is good. It just is, and we have to create meaning for ourselves if we will find meaning at all. There was no original "good" to the universe (we cannot use the word *creation*). What we have is a physical universe that

---

[24]Quoted in Robert N. Bellah, *Religion in Human Evolution: From the Paleolithic to the Axial Age* (Cambridge, MA: Belknap, 2011), 510-11.

is full of beauty, ugliness, peaceful silence, violent explosions, animals, and weather systems. Such a "creation" is meaningless.

What does all of this have to do with the meaning of Christian history? I believe as Christians it may be helpful for a moment to regain the wonder of both a beautiful creation (beginning) and hopeful time (future). We should stop arguing about what cannot be known (how) and affirm afresh the wonder of creation itself (what) and the Creator (who), as the Nicene Creed states: "We believe in one God, the Father almighty, maker of heaven and earth, of all things visible and invisible." Western societies readily accept the concept of time and hope for a better future. Can we also see in a Dennis, or in the 1910 Edinburgh Conference, the long influence of time, of the hope of a creation absolutely dependent on God the Creator? Yes, and yet we also see in the first Students' Lecture on Missions misplaced hope. But there is more. There are other ways the view of time and hope for creation was misused.

TIME AND CHRISTIAN MISSION TODAY

The creation of time, with its movement from chaos to order through fall, redemption, and new creation, continues to be important today for those whose lives are still cyclical. Thus, this view of time (a purpose and a goal for time) continues to be a key issue in Christian witness to Hindus, Buddhists, and others whose lives are bound to the cycles of nature and of reincarnation. Christian missionary encounters with nonlinear-time peoples always turns to a discussion of the meaning of a single God as creator of all things. Creation becomes the main doctrine to be discussed. A few examples should make this clear.

The much persecuted, exiled, and imprisoned Jesuit Alexandre de Rhodes (1593–1660), who worked in both Annam and Cochin China, did a great deal of linguistic work and translation into the Vietnamese script, a script he developed to help common people learn to read.[25] Concerned to present the Christian faith in ways that were understandable or contextually appropriate, de Rhodes's famous catechism was unlike any catechism in Europe at the time.[26] He began his *Eight-Day Catechism* with a long discussion of creation, explaining each day of creation. The whole idea of creation and a single creator God over all of the world and its creatures was a strange and foreign idea to the Vietnamese. Following the lengthy presentation about creation, the *Catechism* then discussed the "three religions" of Vietnam and how they were false, and only then was there a presentation about Jesus.[27] The concept of a single creator was (and is, as we will see) a seismic shift in the consciousness of a people whose myths of creation are largely purposeless and non-historical. Christians, both from the outside as well as local Christians living in Hindu or Buddhist contexts, were very aware of the fundamental contrast of views of creation and therefore of time and future.

Lesslie Newbigin brings the issue to a more contemporary setting: India in the twentieth century. In his book *The Gospel in a Pluralist Society* Newbigin observes that the Tamil language, dominated by Hinduism, had no word for hope.[28] Language and religion are the central elements of any culture; they help us to see a people's view of the sacred and the mundane, of life lived and of powers above. Hinduism in Tamil culture had no need for a word for hope, for the language flowed in the deeply carved wagon-wheel ruts of reincarnation and karma. In contrast to this, creation, time, and fulfillment of time carries with it hope. So, Newbigin says, this is one of the main marks

---

[25]Before the Jesuit work in Vietnamese, all written language was done in the royal and imperial language of Chinese. The Jesuits opened up literacy to all people and de Rhodes's choice of a Latin script became the accepted norm for the Vietnamese language.

[26]For a discussion of the influence of various European Catholic catechisms on de Rhodes's Vietnamese Catechism, see Peter Phan, *Mission and Catechesis: Alexandre de Rhodes and Inculturation in Seventeenth-Century Vietnam* (Maryknoll, NY: Orbis, 1998).

[27]Nearly half of the catechism is on God, creation, and how these beliefs correct the local belief systems in Vietnam.

[28]Lesslie Newbigin, *The Gospel in a Pluralist Society* (Grand Rapids, MI: Eerdmans, 1989), 101.

of a Christian community; it has a future hope. The implications are far reaching: hope gives purpose and motivation for personal progress and communal benevolence. Thus, Christian communities are marked by schools, clinics, and yes, social progress.

In a number of ethnic groups, such as the Karen of Myanmar, there are myths or national stories about a creator God who is far away. It seems that deeply embedded in their cyclical lives was a timeless hope of redemption, or the memory of something that happened long ago but is only vaguely remembered. There are many stories similar to that of the Karen, but the Karen is the one with which I have had some personal contact.[29] I found it so hard to believe, so when I was in Myanmar in the early 1990s, I asked some of my former students, who confirmed the story was very important to them. The Karen myth, passed down from generation to generation, tells that there was a time long ago when the Karen could read, but somehow they had offended the great God. The book (and literacy) was taken away from them. However, a prophecy, given long ago, indicated that sometime in the future a man from far away would come and bring back the sacred book, and they would once again know God the Creator. I have often reflected on the good fortune of those early Baptist missionaries who walked into Karen villages carrying their big Bibles. Needless to say, the Karen were among the first and strongest converts to Christianity in Myanmar. It is interesting that the Karen, living their lives according to the seasons, as worshipers of spirits and marking the cycles of the seasons, had deeply embedded in their psyche and their ethnic mythology an understanding of an event in time that would give them a hope and a future.[30]

This is not a completely empirical study, but it has both been my experience and my observation from history that when Buddhists

---

[29]See Don Richardson, *Eternity in Their Hearts* (Ventura, CA: Regal, 1981).
[30]For the Karen, it was a lost book, and for some West African groups, there is a creator God who has been offended and is now very distant, even though there is no myth of a lost book.

become Christians, they are particularly interested in the stories of creation. Buddhist stories of creation are closer to Gnostic myths, as mysterious error or falling from harmony, which means that creation is a corruption of the ideal or the good. The earliest encounters in China in the modern period, the Jesuits in the late sixteenth and early seventeenth centuries, certainly found this to be true. The two major problems of Christian witness developed into two major controversies: the terms controversy (what term should be used for God) and the rites controversy (whether Christians can participate in ceremonies honoring the ancestors and Confucius). The problem over the term for "God" was that the Chinese had no belief in a creator God. One of the closest terms was the Lord of Heaven (*Tianzhu*), but the concept of heaven was not the same as either the biblical concept of heaven or the Christian concept of God. Heaven did not create and did not directly intervene like the personal Creator God of the Christians. Thus, like the encounter that de Rhodes would later have in Vietnam, and like the encounter of early Christian apologists working in the Roman Empire, teachings about creation were critical. One of Matteo Ricci's great contributions to Chinese culture, as an Italian Christian, was to participate in a neo-Confucianist scholarly debate about the identity of heaven or the Lord of Heaven. Ricci argued that Confucius himself believed in a personal creator God, but his followers did not pass on these teachings. This radical reinterpretation of Confucius developed into a neo-Confucianist school of thought. It was new because of the additional belief in God (or heaven) as creator.

Two other anecdotal pieces of evidence support this importance of creation and therefore the book of Genesis. In 2004 I was teaching a course on Asian Church history in Cambodia, and another professor was teaching a course on the Bible. We were there to teach intensive courses for two weeks to help the new pastors and missionaries (all ninety Khmer students were former Buddhists). I asked the professor what he was teaching on, and he snapped back, "Genesis. That's all they want, more teaching on Genesis." I believe he was a scholar of the Hebrew prophets, so he was hoping that he would get to teach on his area of expertise, but all the Cambodians wanted to learn about was Genesis, mostly creation. It makes perfect sense.

A second story concerns a seminary student our seminary sent to Vietnam to help with training, once again, newer Christian converts from an ethnic group that was formerly all Hindu. He prepared an Old Testament survey course. However, when he returned, he said very clearly, "All their questions were about Genesis. They are fascinated with creation!"

Western Christians are so comfortable with this Christian view of time that it is only when we contrast it to a cyclical or "uncreated" world that we see so clearly the importance of time to Christian existence. In 1552 Francis Xavier wrote the following from Japan:

> The Japanese doctrines teach absolutely nothing concerning the creation of the world, of the sun, the moon, the stars, the heavens, the earth, the sea, and the rest, and do not believe that they have any origin but themselves. The people were greatly astonished on hearing it said that there is one sole Author and common Father of souls, by whom they were created. This astonishment was caused by the fact that in their religious traditions there is nowhere any mention of a Creator of the universe. If there existed one single First Cause of all things, surely, they said, the Chinese, from whom they derive their religion, must have known it. For the Japanese give the Chinese the pre-eminence in wisdom and prudence in everything relating either to religion or to political government. They asked us a multitude of questions concerning this First Cause of all things; whether He were good or bad, whether the same First Cause were the origin of good and of evil. We replied that there exists one only First Cause, and He supremely good, without any admixture of evil.[31]

---

[31]Quoted from William H. McNeil and Mitsuko Iriye, eds., *Modern Asia and Africa*, Readings in World History 9 (New York: Oxford University Press, 1971), 22.

Creation points to a creator as a cause, or more accurately to a first cause.[32] Xavier's apologetic to Japanese (and thus also to Chinese) culture involved origins and the originator before he could talk about redemption and a redeemer.

Creation, and a God who created all including a time continuum, is not just an innovation, but for those from a Hindu or Buddhist heritage, it brings with it the possibility of development, change, progression, and fulfillment. Jesus' coming marks time and humanity. Therefore, the key to time and the key to humanity is found in Jesus Christ, and his coming points back to creation and the God who initiated time, which is being fulfilled.

We could say that Christianity transformed cyclical time and imprinted on it Christian time and progress: the story of salvation and redemption in the Christian calendar. We might say that the Christian view of time converted the cyclical calendar of ancient cultures. For example, the memory of saints draws the Christian back to virtuous Christian living in the past and becomes a model for Christian faith practiced in the present for a future to be transformed. Saints' days are timely as markers for the sanctified life. Many of the saints were martyrs whose lives in time point to a purpose beyond time. Similarly, when Christianity spread into pagan and tribal Europe, some of the cyclical festivals were "baptized,"[33] giving a sense of history to what were previously cyclical reminders of seasonal death and the return of life in the spring. The celebration of new life in spring coincided with the celebration of Jesus rising from the dead. A cyclical festival became a reminder of a particular conquest over death that occurred once and for all in time. Cyclical was transformed to linear.

---

[32]This is an expression of the "cosmological argument" for the existence of God, which goes back to Aristotle, but among Christians Thomas Aquinas was the first to thoroughly argue it, and it became part of the tradition in natural theology.

[33]The meaning here is that local customs or practices are incorporated into the Christian tradition. *Adapted* and *adopted* are words that describe this practice of contextualization of the gospel into local cultures.

When Christianity came into Asian cultures, cyclical and seasonal celebrations were encountered there also. Some of these agrarian festivals had become religious (either Buddhist or related to ancestor worship) and were later Christianized. In Vietnam as well as in Cambodia, there are traditional festivals that mark the cyclical nature of time. For example, there is the first three days of celebration for the new year: *Tất Niên*, the first day, is a day of celebration for the cult of ancestors. The second day, *Giao Thừa*, is dedicated to near relatives. The third day, *Tân Niên*, is dedicated to the dead. Jesuit missionary Alexander de Rhodes adapted this for Christians to celebrate the Trinity on the first days of every new year. Like their Buddhist and Hindu neighbors, they celebrated the new year. But they celebrated it not as a cycle of remembering ancestors but in worship of the Trinity. More to the point here, the celebration of *Tết* (new year) involved erecting tall poles with food attached at the top to feed the ancestors' spirits. De Rhodes adapted this practice for Christians, telling them that Jesus is the bread of life. He taught that the sign of Jesus, a cross, should be placed on the top of Christian poles during *Tết*.

When I taught this to a group of lay leaders in Cambodia, their eyes lit up. Four hundred years later these Cambodian Protestant converts from Buddhism carried out the same practice that a Jesuit told his converts to do in Vietnam. Adapting, connecting, contextualizing, and interpreting were all processes required as the message of God appearing in time became rooted in Khmer life.

MISUSE OF TIME AND REDEMPTION

Not only can the beginning of time be misunderstood, but the hope and goal of time can also be misapprehended, often with tragic consequences. There is a view of time that believes that the future hope can be realized in the church's work today. This was the basic understanding of James Dennis and many church leaders in the progressive era. It has also been the view of many Christian nationalists who see redemption realized in their nation or in Israel. Fulfillment of time is brought about by our human efforts. One way of looking at such a misperception is by giving it the title of an "over-realized eschatology." Such a view rushes ahead of God's plan in time, assuming the promises are now fulfilled fully. But time is not yet fulfilled, and there is still much in the future to be realized. Over-realized eschatologies tend toward quietism on one hand and violence on the other.

There have also been people and movements who saw the hope of the gospel without embracing its humility and patience. In the Reformation period these people were known as revolutionary radicals. People like Thomas Müntzer "seized" time in an effort to usher in a future he and the Allstedt community would control. The results were tragic. The United States has produced many chiliastic, or millennial, as well as Adventist movements with less violence. These are groups that in various ways collapsed the future into the present or reasoned that the eschaton was now to be inaugurated. All of these are misrepresentations of creation, time, and incarnation as we have spoken of it. We mention these because they reveal, even in their overly zealous Christian existence, the centrality of time and hope to Christian faith.

One such movement that brought about the greatest violence and destruction was an Indigenous Christian-influenced movement in China. In the mid-nineteenth century a group of semi-converted Chinese had such a misconception of time, future hope, and (as we will see) the incarnation. As with all of these groups, the personal fulfillment or even personal control over future events was a central theme. This group was known as the Heavenly Kingdom of Great Peace, or the Taipings (1850–1864).[34] The Taipings were a separatist

---

[34]See Jonathan D. Spence, *God's Chinese Son: The Taiping Heavenly Kingdom of Hong Xiuquan* (New York: W. W. Norton, 1996).

kingdom within China that split off and engaged in a long-fought civil war about the same time as the United States Civil War. The Taiping Rebellion (as it is called) was a revolt against the oppressive rule of the Qing, and it was inspired by the apocalyptic Christian teachings of Hong Xiuquan (1814–1864). As with most Christian-influenced renewals, there was a concern for justice. However, this "renewal" movement can and must be judged for its misunderstanding of the message, the Messiah, and the meaning of hope.

Hong was a Hakka Chinese ("guest people") from near Canton who read Chinese materials about Jesus Christ, such as *Good Word for Exhorting the Age* by William Milne's assistant translator and convert, Liang Afa. Hong was influenced by these writings but also by visions, his readings of Confucian texts, selective reading of the recently translated Bible, and of course the social oppression and poverty of late Qing China. Hong's Heavenly Kingdom of Great Peace became a unique Chinese religion based on a realized eschatology: the kingdom of heaven is here, and Hong is the incarnation of the younger brother of Jesus, who is elevated to the place of Heavenly King (*Tian Wang*). He was anxious to bring about the fulfillment of time as described in the Bible. The Heavenly Kingdom developed a massive army of soldiers who memorized the Ten Commandments and copied Bibles by the thousands. The Kingdom was first centered in a strong Hakka region (Guangxi Province, where Karl Gützlaff's Chinese missionaries had made many converts), but then they captured Nanjing with over 750,000 soldiers. For a decade the Kingdom attempted to conquer all of China from this base in the southern Chinese capital. The movement was strongly Biblicist; opposed to idolatry, foot binding, and corruption; and very communal. The Kingdom collapsed as much from internal disorder and murder as from Qing government pressure. It is estimated that between twenty and thirty million people died in this massive civil war, making it one of the most destructive wars in history. It was clear that many of the elements of Christianity found a home in the Chinese heart, but at the core of this movement was the hope that Qing and warlord corruption and violence could be ended and that a Kingdom of Heavenly Peace could become a reality.

Nearly thirty million deaths. The United States' Civil War brought about only two-thirds of one million deaths at about the same time. Unless we have clarity about Christian history, we will have a hard time giving a clear critique to Hong's Heavenly Kingdom or Dennis's earthly kingdom brought on by Christian social progress.

Most Christian-influenced groups that focus on an immediacy of God's fulfillment of time mix their over-realized eschatology with a misunderstanding of incarnation and Christology. For most sects, there is a new messianic person with grandiose personal ambitions. The importance of time and movement in time create the possibility of such chiliastic and apocalyptic movements. The urgency for justice, liberation, or conquest bends such Christian-influenced movements toward violence. The idolatry of a human vision, or the vision of a utopian dream, always tends toward violence.

These chiliastic movements led by a prophetic leader, whether it is Hong Xiuquan, Sun Yung Moon, or others, are usually built around an adoptionist type of savior figure. Since the prophet has accepted a word from God, they are adopted by God as his special son or messenger. Special times require a special savior figure. It is important to be clear that the Christian view of time and incarnation are radically different. The incarnation is the enfleshment of God, who was there from creation. The triune God—Father, Son, and Holy Spirit—brought about the creation that, as we mentioned, was very good. Jesus' incarnation was his taking on that good creation and walking among us. He was from the beginning, not a good person who was adopted to be the son or messenger of God. Avoiding such misreadings of Christianity around the incarnation is one of the reasons for this book.

TIME, INCARNATION, AND BENEVOLENCE

The Christian view of time changes the identity of a people. As we noted earlier, what we remember or think as our history gives us identity and purpose for today. The people who have entered into God's story—the eternal God's secular story—think differently about their identity and purpose. Time's beginning in creation and completion in redemption reorients a person and gives hope. It is such an understanding of the world that helps both to explain and to critique Christian history. People "in" this story are led to live according to this hopeful trajectory in time in their lives.

Missionary work, including schools, Christian hospitals, and literacy programs, makes sense if there is an understanding of human existence in time. This created order is God's playfield. Where time is cyclical, or where creation is myth without history or story without Creator, there is little motivation to change or rearrange the created order. There are cultures and religions that have no concept of time or movement toward fulfillment. In such cultures, work toward improvement is not logical, although at times it does occur. Christian history has this peculiar characteristic: people work to improve the lives of others, push back the frontiers of evil, and redeem the helpless. Movements like the American Education Society, the American Bible Society, or the Little Sisters of the Poor are expressions of Christian hope based on Christian participation in the life of God. We will look at this theme of Christian benevolence in the chapter four, but a simple story will show how normal it is for a person who steps into the narrative of the life of Christ, the incarnate one, to take on such benevolence of love toward others.

When teaching in Cambodia I met a young woman convert whose story so fascinated me I set up time to talk to her over a couple of meals with a translator. Kang Sophal was from a Buddhist family who, along with hundreds of thousands of others, was displaced to develop a utopian agrarian country. Approximately 1.5 million were killed.

Kang's father left the family, and her mother was left to try to survive with three children. Somewhere along the way, they were given a Khmer Bible. With little to no teaching, they read the Bible, and all of them became Christians. But they were Christians without a home. They only had permission to nest under a house built on stilts, living with the pigs and other animals.

Persecution began when the homeowner found out they were Christians. Abuse as well as garbage was thrown at the family. Through a few important miracles, the small family found work, purchased a small plot of land, and had a place to camp out. Then, just when the family was getting settled, Kang began having dreams. Actually, it was the same dream over and over. In her dream, as she described it to me, Jesus, the incarnate God, told her that he was sending her out to tell a far-off village about him. The city, she was told, will become like a city set on a hill, sending out missionaries all over Cambodia. Her mother did not believe her; in fact she ridiculed her and threatened her. Kang obeyed the dream and moved to Beom Tch-Kaw, and for four years began her solitary mission by teaching the children how to read (especially God's Word) and how to follow Jesus.

That is when I met Kang. I spoke to her because she seemed so sad. She was often crying during and after lectures. At our second lunch I found out the reason. She knew she needed training, but she was so lonely in Phenom Penh. She was away from her little congregation of children and a few adults. She would cry for "her children." Her life and story were caught up in the story of life lived for others, suffering, and the persistent hope of glory as she followed Jesus.

We turn now to look to the center of that story, Jesus, and at the important place of suffering in Christian historiography. It is even the center of the story of history itself.

Chapter Three

Cross: The Cruciform and Apostolic Nature of Christianity

May I never boast of anything except the cross of our Lord Jesus Christ, by which the world has been crucified to me, and I to the world.

GALATIANS 6:14

Concerning this salvation, the prophets who prophesied of the grace that was to be yours made careful search and inquiry, inquiring about the person or time that the Spirit of Christ within them indicated when it testified in advance to the sufferings destined for Christ and the subsequent glory.

1 PETER 1:10-11

We proclaim Christ crucified, a stumbling block to Jews and foolishness to Gentiles, but to those who are the called, both Jews and Greeks, Christ the power of God and the wisdom of God.

1 CORINTHIANS 1:23-24

The center of all history,
Your cross and resurrection
Humiliation lifted me,
Into a new creation.

JONATHAN SMITH, MATT MAHER,
AND STEFFANY GRETZINGER

WRITING UP FOR PUBLICATION his L. P. Stone Lectures delivered at Princeton Theological Seminary in 1932–1933, Presbyterian mission statesman and prolific author Robert E. Speer began his preface with these words: "It is not enough to say that the central thing in Christianity is Christ. Christ is not only the center. He is also the beginning and the end."

The title of the lectures was, ironically, titled "The Finality of Jesus Christ." His basis for the lectures was Scripture and the early writings. His context was the growing and broadening ecumenical movement, in which there was a sub-movement away from the center on Jesus Christ to a universal world consciousness.[1] More to the point, his context was the aftermath of the Jerusalem 1928 International Missionary Council meeting where, in the light of advancing secular communism, the theme was "Religions Against Secularization." In the light of such a call by Christian scholars to unite with other religions under a new foundation (or center), Speer wrote a 386-page book defending the centrality (or finality) of Jesus Christ.

---

[1] Robert E. Speer, *The Finality of Jesus Christ* (New York: Fleming H. Revell, 1933). In a very long supplementary note, Speer reveals his motive and purpose for the lectures. The new "center" around which religious unity for world peace would be found was described as this "World Consciousness," but also as "Loyalty," the "ideal and principle" taught by all religions, "Human Solidarity," and "common divinity within ourselves," among other centers or foundations for world peace and harmony (59-62).

Speer's response to a drifting theological center was to go to history. In his estimation the very present threat to Christianity is twofold, and both are related to historical understanding. First, historical interpretations of Christ at the end of the nineteenth and beginning of the twentieth century de-emphasized the historical and earthly nature of Jesus Christ. Similar to other depictions of religious origins and their founders, the story of Jesus was understood to be a myth with purpose, not myth as genuine historical narrative. "They have ranged all the way from the extreme of Drews and Kalthoff and Baur, that Jesus was a pure myth, that there never was a historic Jesus . . . that all the factors necessary to account for [Christianity's] origin can be found in the ancient world without reference to a historical Jesus."[2]

Thus, the first historical question is a matter of historical interpretation about the human being Jesus Christ the Nazarene and his early followers. Speer reaffirms both the historical reality of Jesus as recorded in the Scriptures (and the early church), and he affirms that this historical reality is still meaningful today. In fact, the historical reality not only has meaning but is the interpretive or hermeneutical key for all of history and human life. For Jesus is both historical and eternal: human and divine.

The second historical threat that he writes about is the present historical reality that would re-center history around a common human search. This new center is not a little thing; it completely re-imagines Jesus as one of many who were on a quest to know the divine, or even to discover the divine within. All of this, in Speer's view, is bad history, for it ignores the historical evidence about Jesus, what Jesus said and did, and what people said about Jesus from the beginning.

I was familiar both with the Stone Lectures and the role of Speer in the ecumenical movement and in Presbyterian missionary work.

---

[2]Speer, *Finality of Jesus Christ*, 13.

Historical context is very important. Many of the concerns I am discussing here were central concerns of Speer's close to a century ago.

The unique centrality of Jesus Christ for history was, and continues to be, in doubt. Let me explain. One evening in the 1980s a group of about ten Princeton Theological Seminary PhD students got together to talk about our research, seminars, and our teaching assistant work with professors. I, the most obviously evangelical among an eclectic group of ecumenical Christian scholars, was taking the least Christian sounding course: comparative Buddhist and Christian ethics. Although probably the most conservative among the group, I was studying anthropology, sociology, and the history of religions to prepare to serve in Asia. Others were studying Bible and theology.

I was asked about my Buddhism class and my independent study of Zoroastrianism. In a playfully prodding manner, one of my fellow scholars asked me, "Scott, since you are studying about other religions, what do you think is unique about Christianity? Is there anything unique?" I decided to answer indirectly by turning the tables. "What do you think is unique?"

All types of answers were given, and with each answer (virgin birth, claims to divinity, etc.), I said, "No, you can find a miraculous birth in a number of religions, including Zoroastrianism. Other religious leaders claimed to be god or a son of god, and Apollonius of Tyana was a miracle worker who was worshiped as divine." And so it went on for twenty or thirty minutes. Finally, they asked me again, "Well, Scott, you seem to be one of the most conservative Christians here. You are not a pluralist, are you? What do you think makes Christianity unique, that it is not on the same level as all other religions?"

Everything came in to focus for me that night in the spring of 1985. "If the tomb were not empty, I would go back to painting houses in New England." (I painted houses when I was working on my MDiv in Massachusetts.) "You see, if Jesus, who predicted his death and resurrection, did not really rise from the dead and leave his tomb empty, it is all just story and myth detached from my real earthly life. But if that tomb was really empty, and both prophecies and his teachings are validated, then I will die to my own life and live for him who is the meaning for all of human life."

Well, I may not have been that articulate at the time, but it was a conversation stopper. I think we all preferred to speak in the abstract according to general ethical principles. Something so hard, physical, and historical seemed to be hijacking the theological discourse. Such a belief demands our full attention, even our life. History is important. Understanding the center of history gives meaning to Christianity and to the study of the history of Christianity. I believe it also gives meaning to all of life.

An even stronger statement to this effect has been written by Swiss Jesuit priest and colleague of the *Nouvelle Théologie* school of theology Hans Urs von Balthasar. The *Nouvelle Théologie* scholars sought for theological renewal through the study and translation and publishing of early church writings.[3] Von Balthasar himself worked on Origen, Maximus the Confessor, and Gregory of Nyssa. In his volume titled *A Theology of History*, he underscores as a part of this important Catholic movement (which began to flourish under Nazi dominated Europe) the following:

> For everything is not equidistant from the center, which is the union of God and man, so that we are once again confronted with an analogical relation between different spheres: there are some in which the uniqueness of Christ totally eclipses the abstract general laws, practically replacing them, and others whose relative autonomy persists practically untouched, only having to submit, as it were, to occasional indirect supervision.

---

[3]Among the leaders of this movement, also described by its method, *Ressourcement* ("return to the sources"), were Marie-Dominique Chenu, Yves Congar, Henri de Lubac, Hans Urs von Balthasar, and Jean Daniélou. Many publications came from these scholars, but the most universally appreciated by ecumenical scholars is *Sources Chrétiennes*. It is a bilingual collection of patristic texts, now numbering about 540 volumes, which were originally (beginning in 1942) edited and translated (from Greek, Latin, and Syriac) by the Jesuits Jean Daniélou, Claude Mondésert, and Henri de Lubac.

We find the reason for this analogical relation by looking at the center, Jesus Christ himself. By virtue of the hypostatic union, there is nothing in him which does not serve God's self-revelation. As the center of the world, he is the key to the interpretation, not only of creation, but of God himself.[4]

Von Balthasar continues to explain what this means in terms of theology and liturgy and worship, and in terms of Christian mission. "Even without other proofs of Christ's mission, the concordance between prophecy and fulfillment . . . shows that the whole line of development in the history of salvation is ordered toward himself as its climax."[5] We now turn to look more closely at what it means for there to be a center and meaning to all of history. Then we will look more closely at how this directs our writing and reading of Christian history with a view to the global and missionary nature of Christianity, what I will call "cruciform apostolicity."[6]

WRITING ABOUT A CENTERED-SET RELIGION

Christian history, like the Christian faith itself, must revolve around the central symbol, the cross. It is not possible to give an accurate portrayal of Christian history without in some way holding up the cross as a measure, guide, or interpreter of the faith and even of humanity. By analogy, if we are writing about the history of Islam, or if we are trying to understand Muslim movements today, it would be necessary to refer to Muhammad and some significant events in his life. Muslims are influenced by the life of the founder. When I teach the history of Islam, like most religion professors I begin with the history of the period and spend much more time on the life of Muhammad than on any other period. If you don't understand

---

[4]And we would add that he is the key to the interpretation of all of history. Hans Urs von Balthasar, *A Theology of History* (New York: Sheed and Ward, 1963), 20.

[5]Von Balthasar, *Theology of History*, 21.

[6]Scott W. Sunquist, "*Missio Dei*: Christian History Envisioned as Cruciform Apostolicity," *Missiology* 37, no. 1 (January 2009): 33-46.

Muhammad in his context, you can't understand Islamic history. All Muslims do not follow Muhammad well, and certainly they disagree (strongly and violently) on the meaning of his life and teachings, but knowing about his life is necessary to understand Islam in history. Much of Islamic history is a struggle (jihad) to reclaim the "true" religion in light of the life and teachings of Muhammad.

For Christianity the hermeneutical key is even more dynamic: it is the cross. The cross represents the story of Jesus Christ, and it has become the central symbol of the central event, which has become the central ritual in Christianity. The Eucharist or Last Supper is a visual, tactile, auditory, and olfactory reminder of the cross. The cross symbolizes victory in defeat, humiliation for glory, death for life, and liberation through oppression. The cross also points to a specific suffering for a universal redemption, a particular defeat leading to a universal victory that is both inclusive and unitive. The cross functions as a foundation stone, a touchstone, and a milestone for the Christian. As a foundation stone, it is the beginning and foundation of the Christian. It marks the beginning and the new redeemed identity. As a touchstone, the cross tests the genuineness of a church or individual. The cross functions as the stone that measures the purity of other stones or teachings and institutions. Finally, the cross is a milestone or marker along the Christian way. As a milestone, the cross, in a sense, points the way to Christian faithfulness and toward Christian destiny.

Thus the cross, for any Christian or any Christian community, has a past, present, and future function. Christians throughout history have not always lived in the shadow of the cross, or to use another image, they have often pulled away from the normal Christian orbit around the cross. But even when they do so, we learn something about Christianity at a particular place and time.

I came to the conclusion that the cross was important as a guide in our historical writing and research in 2006. I was asked to give a lecture in a medium-sized university in China, a school that was not one of the former mission colleges but a major university started during Mao's period. The university had a Marxist-Maoist foundation, but in spite of this communist identity, the history department had developed a major focus on religious history, specifically Christianity. In fact, if I remember correctly, I believe that eight of the ten historians teaching in the new master's degree program were studying the history of Christianity. All had earned PhDs, mostly from European universities. Their interest was not just in Christianity in China, but they were studying Christianity throughout its history and throughout the world.

With this kind of background, why was I asked to come and lecture? After close to two decades of studying Christianity, they were beginning to realize that studying Christianity was different from studying Marxist ideology, military history, or the history of international trade. Marxist-materialist approaches did not work when applied to the study of Christian history. My assignment was to outline in two three-hour lectures how to study Christianity. I was curious about this great interest in Christianity in a history department, so I asked three of the students. They all said it has to do with developing a moral society. Their study and interests were motivated by love for China and China's future. They wanted much of what Christianity offers or seems to produce as a byproduct. Or they wanted the healing power of Christianity without taking the strong medicine. These Chinese scholars saw the same evidence that James Dennis saw: we observe social progress when people become Christians. Chinese scholars were coming to the conclusion that they would like to find out how Christianity has functioned in their history to bring about moral and social progress.

Some Chinese scholars understand what it means to bring about such "progress." I mean they understand the cost of having such a precious byproduct. They have come to embrace not only the teachings of the Beatitudes but also the *teacher* of the Beatitudes. For others, they want the results, but they do not understand that results require certain commitments and beliefs. One scholar I interviewed did his PhD work in Rome and focused on Christianity in the late Roman Empire. I asked him why he studied that period, since most Chinese are studying Christianity in China. His comment was quiet, clear, and direct: "Because we are just like Rome in late antiquity." He may not be exactly correct, but he expressed well the sentiment of many. Other Chinese scholars told me that China was becoming a powerful empire without a moral center. I was overwhelmed by their zeal to understand Christian history without knowing much about its founder and its understanding of history.

My point, however, is not about the scholars but what I learned about Christian history through my interaction with the professors and graduate students. I was trying to explain that studying Christian history required certain sensitivities. I asked myself, "What does it mean for a communist—a real Marxist materialist—to study Christian history?" There must be an interpretive key, or else you will impose a method and assumptions that are foreign to Christianity. By analogy, if you are studying the history of a bank or accountancy firm, you must know what banks are for, and what the purpose of accounting is. You will need to know about local and international laws regarding banking and accounting.

After spending the last decade or so following various movements and expressions of Christianity, I was prepared for this lecture. Although at times certain cultural forms of Christianity have become scholastic and bounded (this and not this), for the most part, Christianity must be understood as more centered than bounded set.[7]

---

[7]*Bounded set* and *centered set* are terms that were originally used for mathematics but have been picked up by anthropologists in recent decades. Like all interpretive grids, it has limited application, but it is helpful to raise up basic approaches of cultures and religions. The application of what is actually a cognitive category to anthropology and religions was pioneered by Paul G. Hiebert in "Conversion, Cultures and Cognitive Categories," *Gospel in Context* 1, no. 4 (1978): 24-29.

Boundaries do develop, but they do not define Christianity. In fact, the center must define the boundaries. I believe this is classic Pauline and Petrine theology. Each of their letters begins by talking about the meaning of Jesus and *then* goes on to talk about practices that follow. The central teaching (e.g., Phil 1; Col 1; Eph 1–2) is followed by moral and ethical teachings (boundaries) based on the center.

I asked the students and professors a question. "What do we see on most every church?"

Three of the forty or so in the class raised their hands. One bright young lady in the front row rose, answered, "A cross," bowed, and sat down.

"Good," I said, "and what does a cross represent?"

Again she raised her hand (as if she were the class spokesperson), stood up, and clearly said, "I have no idea, sir."

And this was the rub. The central historical anchoring of Christianity was not understood. They were trying to understand motives, decisions, and writings without the key. I later found out that of the forty or so graduate students, only one was a Christian. Christian history does not cohere or make sense without an understanding of its center.

And so I explained as quickly as I could that Christians believe that God came to earth, showed and told people how to live, and was rejected and killed by being nailed to a cross. The students were madly writing all of this down. Christians believe that Jesus, God in the flesh, died for our sins, was buried in a grave, and then rose from the dead and continues to call people to trust him. He empowers his followers to lead his life on earth today. It was a quick statement of generic Christian belief that I thought my father, my professor, my Catholic publisher, and Pentecostal Singaporean students could all affirm. Before I finished, the department head, a soon-to-be Communist Party member himself, jumped to his feet and started speaking in highly animated, extremely rapid Mandarin. After two or three minutes of this—a period of time when I was imagining being ushered out of the country quickly for such an unguarded kerygmatic outburst, or possibly spending my remaining days in an unknown prison in far-off Sichuan—suddenly the professor turned to me and gave me a very restrained East Asian hug.

"Thank you," he exclaimed. "I have been trying to get them to understand that if you don't know about Jesus, you can't really study the history of Christianity. Christians are always trying to follow Jesus, right? How can they learn more about Jesus?" I gave him my New Testament and encouraged them to read it, and we went out to lunch.

CRUCIFORM APOSTOLICITY

The cross does not stand alone. The cross—seen in the Gospel accounts, in the theology of Paul and Peter, and throughout most of the church's history—is integrally related to the sending nature of God and the apostolic, or "sent," nature of the church.

I believe that these twin characteristics of cross and mission describe two of the three core characteristics that are needed to see and evaluate Christian movements as well as our own local church: mission and suffering, or cruciform apostolicity. When Christian movements forget the missionary nature of their calling, they misrepresent the Savior. When churches and individual Christians avoid suffering (misreading it as a sign God is redirecting us), Christ himself is being denied. Jesus addresses this very clearly when he speaks about his future and the future of his followers:

> Then he began to teach them that the Son of Man must undergo great suffering, and be rejected by the elders, the chief priests, and the scribes, and be killed, and after three days rise again. He said all this quite openly. And Peter took him aside and began to rebuke him. But turning and looking at his disciples, he rebuked Peter and said, "Get behind me, Satan! For you are setting your mind not on divine things but on human things." He called the crowd with his disciples, and said to them, "If any want to

become my followers, let them deny themselves and take up their cross and follow me." (Mk 8:31-34)

There is a direct connection between the suffering and rejection of Jesus Christ and our own life in Christ. The church is to be the community of people in Christ who have also denied themselves and taken up his identity of suffering for others. Christianity is a missionary religion that, for all of its confusion with colonialism and international trade, promoted a new humanity in Christ and worked to see it enfleshed in local communities. There is a missionary nature to Christianity that is carried out in humility and suffering.

Thus, Christian existence is symbolized by the cross, and the cross points to humiliation and suffering on behalf of others. However, the cross paradoxically points to glory for the nations. "And I, when I am lifted up from the earth, will draw all people to myself" (Jn 12:32). "Lifted up" is not like an awards ceremony; it is public torture and death. Five times this concept of Jesus being lifted up on the cross is repeated. Public torture leading to death is the path to glory for all the nations. It is not just that the center of Christianity is Jesus; it is the cross and its suffering and humiliation that reveals God to us and in the same breath invites us to follow. The cross has a global, even cosmic meaning.

The cross is the climax of the redemption story of which the resurrection and ascension are the denouement. At the other end of the redemption story is the incarnation, also a type of suffering, or at least a self-emptying event. The incarnation story is unique in religions. We noted in chapter two the importance of the doctrine of creation *ex nihilo* and the concept of time—a novel concept for most people. In a similar way, the incarnation stands in radical contrast to a more common type of visitation, that of avatar, reincarnation, or emanation. Christian incarnation is the coming into creation of the perfect and wholly other Creator, YHWH. Misunderstood by many in the first centuries, Jesus was not an emanation or lesser being from God, for God is not creation, and nothing of creation is God. Jesus is sent from the heart of the Creator God and is therefore the first missionary, and we are his continuing work. Thus the cross, as the center of the redemption story, points back to the missionary work of the incarnation and points forward to the death of death and the redemption of all. Christianity is a missionary faith in the pattern of its Lord, but it is also a suffering faith, again in the pattern of its Lord.

It is imperative that we hold on to both of these—incarnation and suffering or apostolicity and passion—lest we run the risk of denying Christ in one of two ways. If we do not embrace the missionary nature of Christianity, we mock the love of God, which by its very nature is not something to be held or stored for ourselves. By its very nature love is to be shared, even at the cost of one's profession, popularity, or life. "As the Father has sent me, so send I you" (Jn 20:21) is not an endearing motivational poster. No, Jesus, here in John 20 (and again in Mt 28:16-20; Mk 16:15-16; Lk 24:45-49; and Acts 1:8) is expressing the doctrine of adoption. We are adopted by God as his children, and thus we inherit, both in duty and reward, what belongs to the Father. Our sending is like our inheritance, our participation in the life of God. "God was reconciling the world to himself in Christ, not counting people's sins against them. And he has committed to us the message of reconciliation. We are therefore Christ's ambassadors, as though God were making his appeal through us" (2 Cor 5:19-20 NIV).

On the other end of the story, if we do not embrace the suffering Savior, we run the risk of living and promoting a cheap faith, and we will be sidestepping the "stumbling block" that has led many astray. "But we proclaim Christ crucified, a stumbling block for the Jews and foolishness to Gentiles" (1 Cor 1:23). From the very earliest followers of the historic Jesus of Nazareth, it was understood that living and preaching a crucified God would cause suffering and persecution. And persecution did come for those who held on to the dual identity of Jesus as Lord (God) and as suffering servant (man). For those citizens of late antiquity, it was much easier, or more tolerable, to compromise on his lordship or his suffering. And so numerous "choices" (heresies)[8] developed that either denied his full humanity and therefore his suffering or denied he was fully God. The cross as the symbol of the suffering, incarnate God, led to the great suffering of many of his early followers and has been a theme throughout Christian history.

I would rather not be talking about suffering, but it is necessary if we are going to develop a historical approach that is true to the religion itself and gives us a perspective for understanding and evaluating Christian movements in history. The doctrine of suffering is not just a matter of pain for purity; it is much more profound. In Jesus' life we learn that humility overcomes arrogance, suffering overcomes death, and power is overcome by humiliation. "Do not repay evil for evil" is not a bumper sticker; it is part of the *via dolorosa* of Christian faith, and it is a path that eventually leads to glory (chapter four). Remembering these two entwined principles of the missionary nature of Christianity and the suffering nature of the church makes it possible to see the precious red thread in history and to make judgments regarding imitations and misuses of the Christian label. We must make accurate judgments. When Christianity is spread through domination, power, coercion, or deceit, we can critique decisions that were made in light of this core doctrine of suffering. We do not have to defend the *reconquista*, the crusades, the slave trade, or evangelists who promise health or wealth. But if we do *not* have clarity about suffering seen in humiliation and self-emptying, it will be difficult to critique those gospels of power, oppression, or conquest.

---

[8]The Greek word for heresy (*hairesis*) means "choice."

CROSS: SUFFERING AND BEING SENT

When writing an introductory volume on Christian mission, I took a trinitarian approach, which was mostly indebted to my training in Bible and history. History dominated the volume. But in drawing on history from a missiological approach, I was overwhelmed by the suffering of those engaged in mission. On the other hand, I was also struck by the amazing changes that took place in societies as a result of Christian mission.

Although it is not popular to note positive results of Western missions today, one award-winning political science article underscores the positive side of the missionary enterprise over the past few centuries. Robert Woodberry's 2012 article, which summed up years of global research, studied the influence of Christian missions on the development of "liberal democracies" in the world.[9] In particular his focus was on conversionary Protestants (CPs). These are Protestants who intentionally sought to bring people to faith in Jesus Christ and were not exclusively setting up schools or hospitals. In studying CPs his research team looked for the long-term influence on measurable variables that were necessary for the development of liberal democracies: mass education, mass printing, newspapers, voluntary organizations, social reform, and so on. In addition, he measured the literacy rates, lifespans, infant mortality, and other measures of standards of living for regions in Africa, Oceania, Latin America, and Asia. He asked the question, Did Christian missions have a lasting impact, decades or even a century later, even if there are few or no missionaries serving today? The results were later summarized in an article in *Christianity Today*.[10] In virtually every measurement, local communities were better off today because of the service of CPs in their

---

[9]Robert Woodberry, "The Missionary Roots of Liberal Democracy," *American Political Science Review* 106, no. 2 (2012): 244-74.
[10]Robert Woodberry, "The World the Missionaries Made," *Christianity Today*, January/February 2014, 34-41.

region.[11] It did not matter whether their work was literacy, translation, medical, church planting and evangelism, or establishing schools.

This one article provides extensive empirical evidence for what I had been observing less systematically over the previous thirty years that indicated both the great suffering and remarkable social consequences of missionary work. Missionaries who were the first to bring modern medicine, literacy, or clean water to isolated regions suffered greatly. In some regions, such as central Africa, the mortality rate of missionaries and their families was extremely high. The great and long-lasting results of Protestant missionaries came with a very high cost.[12]

I decided on the dual concept of suffering and glory to describe the experience of the apostolic life of the church and what was so clearly taught in Scripture.[13] In fact, once I settled on this as a theme for the whole volume, it became clear that this was how the early church understood Jesus' mission and the church's mission. Here are some Scriptures that describe this sub-theme of our focus on the cross as the center of all history, with added emphases.

- Was it not necessary that the Messiah should *suffer* these things and then enter into his *glory*? (Lk 24:26)

- But in those days, after that *suffering*, the sun will be darkened, and the moon will not give its light, and the stars will be falling from heaven, and the powers in the heavens will be shaken. Then they will see "the Son of Man coming in clouds" with great power and *glory*. (Mk 13:24-26)

---

[11]This is not the place to explain why it is that CPs had a consistent positive social influence, which was not necessarily true for Roman Catholic missions. Part of the difference can be translation. Roman Catholics, focusing on the Latin language, did not do as much grassroots work in literacy until after Vatican II. See Woodberry, "Missionary Roots," 250, for an explanation of the lower rates of literacy for Roman Catholic regions, except where they were competing with CPs.

[12]There are many studies, but as an example see Benjamin Diara, Johnson Diara, and George C. Nche, "The Nineteenth-Century European Missionaries and the Fight Against Malaria in Africa," *Mediterranean Journal of Social Sciences* 4, no. 16 (2013): 89-96.

[13]Scott Sunquist, *Understanding Christian Mission: Participation in Suffering and Glory* (Grand Rapids, MI: Baker Academic, 2013).

- The Son of Man must undergo great *suffering*, and be rejected by the elders, chief priests, and scribes, and be killed, and on the third day be raised. . . . Those who are ashamed of me and of my words, of them the Son of Man will be ashamed when he comes in his *glory* and the *glory* of the Father and of the holy angels. (Lk 9:22, 26)

- [Paul was] explaining and proving that it was necessary for the Messiah to *suffer* and to rise from the dead, and saying, "This is the Messiah, Jesus whom I am proclaiming to you." (Acts 17:3, referring to Lk 24:26)

- [Paul said] that the Messiah must *suffer*, and that, by being the first to rise from the dead, he would proclaim light both to our people and to the Gentiles. (Acts 26:23, again referring to Lk 24:26, where glory is understood as the resurrection, and suffering and glory are linked to mission)

- And if [we are] children, then [we are] heirs, heirs of God and joint heirs with Christ—if, in fact, we *suffer* with him so that we may also be *glorified* with him. (Rom 8:17)

- We have gained access to this grace in which in which we stand; and we boast in our hope of sharing the *glory* of God. And not only that, but we also boast in our *sufferings*. (Rom 5:2-3)

- I pray therefore that you may not lose heart over my *sufferings* for you; they are your *glory*. (Eph 3:13)

- But we do see Jesus, who for a little while was made lower than the angels, now crowned with *glory* and honor because of the *suffering* of death. (Heb 2:9)

There are many other places where we see the clear identity of the Messiah as one who suffered in order to attain glory, and his followers are invited to participate in his life of suffering for God's glory.

However, the place where it is made most clear is in 1 Peter. First Peter is a good place to look at the dual themes of suffering and glory in the apostolic nature of Christianity at the center of history. Written not to a local church or to a particular community of Christians in a town, Peter addresses exiles, people who have been dispersed because of persecution (1 Pet 1:1; 2:11). The apostolic nature of their faith is made clear in Peter's reminder that holiness is for the sake of Christian witness to others. "Conduct yourselves honorably among the Gentiles, so that, though they malign you as evildoers, they may see your honorable deeds and glorify God when he comes to judge. . . . Always be ready to make your defense to anyone who demands from you an accounting for the hope that is in you, yet do it with gentleness and reverence" (1 Pet 2:12; 3:15-16). Thus, the sent nature of the faith is understood both in the fact that the recipients of the letter were dispersed (forced out) and that they were to model the faith and speak about the faith where they have arrived.

Although the concept of suffering, both of Jesus and of Jesus' body, is mentioned over sixteen times in the letter, it is in the first chapter where the clearest connection between suffering and glory is presented.[14] In the opening verses, the concept of suffering and death is in the background. Peter writes about the wonderful salvation that Christians have, and it is really quite extensive. But in the background, even before he mentions suffering and death, there are hints of the cost of this salvation. "Sprinkled with his blood" (1 Pet 1:2) refers to sacrifices prescribed in the law for purification from sins. The priests were sprinkled with blood from the sacrifice, and Peter says that Christians are now a "royal priesthood" (1 Pet 2:9). Then in 1 Peter 1:3 Peter talks about resurrection from the dead. Resurrection is a great result, but it happens through death. In 1 Peter 1:4 he mentions an inheritance, which of course benefits a person only upon death. My inheritance does not really benefit anyone yet. So even though 1 Peter 1:3-9 focuses on the precious and undefiled inheritance which we have, the cost is not far from his mind.

---

[14]Suffering is found in the following passages: 1 Pet 1:6, 11; 2:19-24; 3:14, 17-18; 4:15-16, 19; 5:1, 9-10.

Then Peter turns in 1 Peter 1:10 to look at the miraculous nature of this salvation or inheritance gift. Its value is seen in that it was prophesied long ago through special revelation to the prophets. Even angels are excluded from something so precious. As Peter describes it, the prophets were searching to find out about the coming of the Messiah. The confirmation that they received, or the key to knowing who the Messiah really is, was the confluence of suffering and glory in one man. As Peter expresses it, they inquired about the person or time that "the Spirit of Christ within them indicated when it testified in advance to the sufferings destined for Christ and the subsequent glory" (1 Pet 1:11). It was the Spirit of Christ pointing to Christ's incarnation. The one clearest reference that Peter would be certainly thinking about is Isaiah 53:3-5.

> He was despised and rejected by others;
>   a man of suffering and acquainted with infirmity;
> and as one from whom others hide their faces
>   he was despised, and we held him of no account.
> Surely he has borne our infirmities
>   and carried our diseases;
> yet we accounted him stricken,
>   struck down by God, and afflicted.
> But he was wounded for our transgressions,
>   crushed for our iniquities;
> upon him was the punishment that made us whole,
>   and by his bruises we are healed.

Jesus, the one who suffered to bring the glory of the redemption of humanity, has become the forerunner for us. He is our pattern for life that is redeemed. We also can expect to travel the road of suffering for the revelation of glory and joy. In 1 Peter 3 Peter reminds these people living in exile that they can expect to suffer for doing good. "But even if you do suffer for doing what is right, you are blessed" (1 Pet 3:14). "For it is better to suffer for doing good, if suffering should be God's will, than to suffer for doing evil. For Christ also suffered" (1 Pet 3:17-18).

Although 1 Peter has the most thorough and clear statement of participating in Christ's suffering in our obedience to his commission, the Gospel of John has the most succinct: "And I, when I am lifted up from the earth, I will draw all people to myself" (Jn 12:32). The mission of God (drawing all people to Jesus) is carried out through the violent death of Jesus on the cross (lifted up). Thus, the ultimate mission of Jesus, and the commission of the church to reach all the nations of the world, is accomplished through the suffering of Jesus on the cross. Again, we can say that Jesus' passion and mission are of one fabric: cruciform apostolicity.

SUFFERING AND CROSS AS A HERMENEUTIC GUIDE FOR THE HISTORIAN

Now we turn to look at some examples from Christian history to see how this principle of suffering and the cross helps to guide us in our study and how it helps to interpret the meaning of Christian history. In doing so, we are being selective. These are vignettes that illustrate what might be seen as normative Christianity, the faith that germinates in the soil of Scripture and extends to all nations according to the cruciform apostolicity we have described. There is no perfect mission and no perfect Christian story from history. These are types that point back to the archetype, Jesus.

We start with an extreme example, and that is Mother Teresa (Anjezë Gonxhe Bojaxhiu, 1910–1997). She is an extreme example because some of this history we will talk about is unprovable visions and voices from Jesus. In most Christian history we do not base our story on the miraculous.[15] In Teresa's case the main story revolves around her intimate relationship with Jesus and then perceived abandonment by Jesus. Having sensed God's call from an early age to be a missionary,

---

[15]Constantine's heavenly vision of the Chi-Rho coupled with the audible words *In hoc signo vinces* ("Conquer in this sign") is one of the exceptions. Most histories downplay the miraculous and focus on verifiable human events and writings.

she then vowed "not to refuse him anything." She was guided by God's absolute love in all she did, saying, "Don't look for big things, just do small things with great love. . . . The smaller the thing, the greater must be our love."[16] Such absolute devotion to Jesus turned to an even deeper commitment to the poor during her thirty-sixth year of life. She had intimate conversations with "My Jesus . . . my own Jesus," as she called him. These conversations with Jesus were expressed in letters to her confessor in sentences such as the following:

> I want Indian nuns victims of My love, who would be Mary and Martha. . . . I want free nuns covered with My poverty of the cross. . . . Now I want to act—let Me do it—My little spouse—My own little one. Do not fear—I shall be with you always.—You will suffer and you suffer now—but if you are my own little spouse—the spouse of the Crucified Jesus—you will have to bear these torments on your heart. . . . My little one—come—come—carry me into the holes of the poor.—Come be My light.—I cannot go alone—They don't know Me—so they don't want Me. You come—go amongst them, carry Me with you into them.—How I long to enter into their holes—their dark unhappy homes. Come be their victim.—In your immolation [sacrifice]—in your love for Me—they will see Me, know Me, want Me. Offer more sacrifices—smile more tenderly, pray more fervently and all the difficulties will disappear.[17]

This is only part of the story of her voluntary suffering for Jesus. After this year of conversations with Jesus, there was nothing. No voice. She did not even sense the presence of God. Not for the next year, the next decade, not at all for forty-nine years. Yet she followed the clear instructions of Jesus to the end, and she was awarded the Nobel Peace Prize in 1979 at the age of sixty-nine. Sent by Jesus to care for the poor and dying, her "being sent" was in suffering and even loneliness: cruciform apostolicity.

---

[16]These were her instructions to her sisters on October 30, 1981. Mother Teresa and Brian Kolodiejchuk, *Mother Teresa: Come Be My Light; The Private Writings of the "Saint of Calcutta"* (New York: Doubleday, 2007), 34.

[17]Mother Teresa and Kolodiejchuk, *Mother Teresa*, 48-49, 98.

We turn now from this one solitary life to Christian history in earlier periods. As we noted earlier, the missionaries to Africa suffered greatly in bringing the gospel and improving the health in various regions. I have not seen a definitive study, but I believe along the coasts of West Africa and in Southeast Asia, missionaries on average lived six months to eight years after landing. Many packed their belongings in coffins to save time later. Europeans were not fit for African diseases, just like Central Americans and Pacific Islanders were not suited for European diseases.

Another historic example of this hermeneutic guide for history is a story from the Pacific Islands. Tahitians were minding their own business when Europeans in their large, dirty ships and famished libidos landed on their islands bringing rum and venereal disease. Rum became so addictive for the people that many of the cultures of the Pacific Islands were threatened. One historian has remarked that they nearly bathed in it. A Congregational missionary remarked that there was barely any time to talk to King Liholiho of Hawaii when he was sober. Again, the Polynesians were minding their own business when all of this came upon them. Colonialism, in the guise of "free trade," brought corruption in these societies.

Missionaries, however, chose to go and take the risks of life and health by living with local people. They were also risking being misunderstood by the local people as being the same as the sailors and traders with the same morals and purposes. Sailors and traders are not missionaries, but to local people they are almost identical. But not all of the missionaries who brought the gospel to the Pacific Islanders were European.

The missionaries that first arrived in Hawaii were not Americans but Tahitians. Those Tahitians also took great risks in bringing the gospel to the Hawaiians. It is a long way to paddle and sail from Tahiti to the "Sandwich Islands," but once the Tahitians learned about Jesus Christ, they, as adopted sons and daughters of powerful

Atua (YHWH), were compelled to continue his mission to their distant neighbors. When the Americans arrived a few years later, they depended on the newly literate Tahitians to help them with the local language. It was a little humiliating but greatly satisfying to find that there were already Pacific Islander Christians to help out.

I do not want to prooftext my point by selectively only telling stories that prove my theory, so let's look at a few worst-case scenarios to see if this missional-sacrificial or cruciform apostolicity holds true. Is this really foundational in understanding Christianity in history? The next examples show that even when the context seems to discredit the message and the messengers, the concept of cruciform apostolicity remains as a mark of gospel integrity.

What could be worse for Christian mission than Europeans and North Americans trying to convert people they have enslaved? Enslaving people and then telling them about the "love of God" seems like a worst-case scenario. Or what about the terrible situation where the British were trying to convert the very people to whom they were selling opium in China? Remember the concept of the thin red thread from the introduction? My point in using that image is that in the worst of situations, with the least support or in the most compromised of situations, the cruciform life of Christ is still carried into the world with transforming power. But it comes with much suffering and often being misunderstood.

There are a number of remarkable stories in Christian history, but the conversion of African enslaved people has to be among the most tragic and surprising. Brought over in the most horrible of conditions, generally treated as animals, Africans were evangelized by other people and ended up with a larger percentage of Christians than the Europeans and white Americans who evangelized them. So we must look at the terrible suffering of Africans. This is the immediate context of their encounter with the suffering God. Expressed this way, we can begin to see the possibility of a redemptive message being understood by enslaved people.

Missionaries working with those who were enslaved were also working in the most compromised of contexts. So there was a double suffering involved in this situation: Europeans and North Americans brought tremendous suffering on Africans captured and transported against their will to the Americas. Missionaries were going against the social tide by doing missionary work among the slaves. Some missionaries were imprisoned or deported for teaching enslaved people to read. Slave owners knew that revolutions developed from informed and educated oppressed people.[18] But Christian missions required the very thing slave owners feared: education and better living conditions.

A brief look at the Caribbean "slave evangelism" story will help in our understanding of the missionary and suffering nature of Christianity in compromised contexts. During the eighteenth century in the Caribbean, sugar was king. This meant that the plantation owners had to increase the labor pool to keep up with the European and North American demand for sugar. Plantations became very large, and production increased with larger fields, advances in technology, and more enslaved people. In 1775, the Island plantations of Jamaica had an estimated 19,000 Europeans (mostly British), with an estimated 193,000 enslaved people.[19] On most of the islands, the ratio of owners to the enslaved was one to ten.

Most of the Europeans who settled in the Caribbean were there for the money to be made. Their Christian convictions and spiritual life

---

[18]One of the greatest abolitionists of the nineteenth century was Frederick Douglass. While Frederick was still an enslaved child, the wife of his owner began teaching him to read the Bible. When the slave owner found out he put an end to it, but he was too late. Reading the Bible, singing Methodist hymns, and reading abolitionist material helped to create one of the greatest orators of the nineteenth century. See David W. Blight, *Frederick Douglass: Prophet of Freedom* (New York: Simon and Schuster, 2018).

[19]Jan Rogonzinski, *A Brief History of the Caribbean: From the Arawak and Carib to the Present*, rev. ed. (New York: Plume, 2000), 116.

generally were at a very low ebb. With few bishops ever in the area, Caribbean societies ran according to the Erastian principle, whereby the ecclesiastical powers were subordinate to the secular powers. This Erastian social order increased in all of Latin America in the eighteenth century. In the British colonies, the governor of each colony functioned as a sort of lay bishop called "the Ordinary." Governors and lay leaders were of one mind in their responsibility of upholding social order, especially the protection of "property rights." This meant that the church was implicated in protecting the rights of slaveholders rather than the enslaved people. Governors were loyal to the laws of England and faithful to promote only the Church of England. Although the eighteenth century was a period of promotion of the "rights of man" in Europe, in most of the colonies, such rights belonged only to the aristocracy. Conversion of the "African and Natives" was enjoined in theory, but little was done to actually bring Christian teachings to local people or to slaves in ways they could understand.[20] Royal policy supported evangelization of the enslaved, but the local "West Indian plantocracy" was much more resistant toward all who would take up missionary work among enslaved people.

Into this mix of political and economic struggles in the Caribbean came the earliest Protestant missionaries, whose goal was to plant churches or Christian communities among the local and African populations. Most of the pioneers were Moravians (*Herrnhuter Brüdergemeine*). Rebecca Protten, the Afro-Caribbean evangelist and the first woman of color known to be ordained (1746), was a part of the global ministry of the *Brüdergemeine*. In fact Rebecca was taught to read by a kindly slave holder and was given the freedom to become

---

[20]"The royal instructions begun in 1690 were repeated decade after decade requiring each governor, 'with the assistance of the council and assembly to find out the best means to facilitate and encourage the conversion of Negroes and other slaves to the Christian religion.' Sometimes the stipulation was added: 'wherein you are to have a due caution and regard to the property of the inhabitants and safety of the colony.'" Arthur Charles Dayfoot, *The Shaping of the West Indian Church, 1492–1962* (Gainesville: University Press of Florida, 1998), 101.

a traveling evangelist, and she was the welcome translator for the German *Herrnhutters* when they arrived.

The first Moravians began their work in the Caribbean in 1732. Although there had been Protestant Anglicans, Puritans, and Huguenots in the Caribbean for over a hundred years, the Moravians came with the express purpose of reaching out to the majority population: Africans. The first Moravian missionaries were chosen by lot: Leonard Dober (1706–1766), a potter, and David Nitschmann (1696–1772), a ship's carpenter, left for St. Thomas on August 21, 1732.

The Moravian work, especially in the Caribbean, was a unique development in modern mission. Their sole purpose was to reach out to enslaved Africans. They arrived not as trained theologians, priests, or monks but as carpenters, potters, printers, and other skilled laborers. They planned to use these skills both for personal support and to help the impoverished and enslaved Africans. Unlike the Roman Catholic *reductiones*, the Moravians did not go out to gather people into communities to Christianize them. The Moravians were working with sedentary people who were enslaved, not semi-nomadic Indigenous people, so in a reverse fashion, they settled down with those who were enslaved. Their ecclesial location or identity was somewhat fluid, for they weren't exactly Lutherans, but they did have bishops, and the mission-minded Count Zinzendorf almost functioned as a pope. They sent people out to serve in Pentecostal fashion, praying and trusting and listening for a word from the Lord. Within the first generation (by 1739), they were sending out married couples, even to very difficult and dangerous regions like the Caribbean.

Death and suffering came early to these missionaries. When their colleagues were dying in the Caribbean tropics, rather than retreating, the Moravian leader himself, Zinzendorf, traveled to the Caribbean to investigate and to plan for future work. Death proved to be too small an enemy for the Moravian missionaries. After just two years in St. Thomas, a new group of Moravians was sent to build up the work, but they only added to the list of Christian martyrs. Within a year, ten of the eighteen had died. In 1736 Herrnhut sent out another eleven missionaries, but nine died within the year. The survivors were called back. Then, after regrouping and praying for guidance, another nine missionaries were sent out, including two married couples. All of these early pioneers had to suffer criticism, and in some cases imprisonment, from other Europeans. The Moravian commitment to and identification with the Africans was seen as threatening to the European landed aristocracy and their oppressive economic order.

Of the few that survived in these early years, their work proved to be very fruitful. Frederick Martin (1704–1750) came to St. Thomas in 1736 to carry on the work Dobler (who had to return to Germany to be ordained) had pioneered. Martin was stronger and healthier than others, in part because he had already suffered for his faith in Moravia. He began his work by living among the enslaved and starting conversations to learn the language and to share the Christian faith in a more personal manner. Martin was ordained in absentia, which caused much criticism, but by 1737 he had started the first Moravian Congregation in the Americas, an Afro-Caribbean congregation. It was called New Herrnhut. The baptism of the first three enslaved people that same year may have caused a great deal of opposition from the Reformed cleric, Pastor Borm, but the imprisonment (in part because of his refusal to take an oath) highlighted the Moravian work and brought great respect for these self-supporting Christian workers. Frederick Martin became known as the Moravian "Apostle to the Negroes." Christianization continued in the shadow of slavery, and eventually Christians who had formerly been enslaved were the pioneers in the transformation of Christianity in the West. Lamin Sanneh, Andrew Walls, and others are clear that it was those who had been freed from slavery and who then received an education who had the greatest impact on the end of the slave trade. Afro-Caribbeans are much more likely to be Christian than white Americans even up to the present time.

We don't have the space to look at China in depth, but suffice it to say that nineteenth-century missionaries in China were under an equally difficult contextual missionary setting. Chinese rulers were clear that they did not want opium imported to their country. By the early nineteenth century it was obvious that opium was destructive of the economy and society. However, the British had turned a trade deficit into a huge surplus by growing opium in India and exporting it to China. The Qing Dynasty was in decline but insisted on keeping out foreign empires. Only a few treaty ports were open to foreigners. Not only foreigners were excluded from China, but the religion of foreigners, Christianity, had also been outlawed as early as 1721 by Emperor Kangxi.

However, pressure from expanding empires of Europe meant both trade and missionaries began to arrive. Robert Morrison's (1782–1834) earliest work in translating the Bible (beginning in 1807) was all illegal. Both learning Chinese himself and teaching his Chinese assistants to read the Bible and pray were illegal. Soon the same ships that unloaded casks of opium were also bringing men and women proclaiming the good news of salvation from sin. Chinese, like Africans, proved able to distinguish multi-national traders from missionaries. Conversions were slow at first, but the literary work, schools, and hospitals established small but widely spread Christian communities throughout China. It is true that the great growth of Christianity under communism and especially after the death of Chairman Mao has been the result of Chinese evangelists and pastors. However, the Christian work of those Chinese evangelists and missionaries finds its heritage in Western missionaries, who were often confused with opium traders. The faithfulness of Chinese Christians even after decades of oppression and persecution has resulted in the present situation where, on a weekly basis, there are likely more Chinese than Europeans who worship Jesus Christ.

BETRAYAL: A SUFFERING PATH TO GLORY

One final story illustrates sending and suffering in Christian history. Teaching at a seminary in the United States in the late 1990s, I helped to establish a center that would send seminary students to work alongside missionaries or national Christians in regions that were under-evangelized. We were looking to send students to regions that might be considered frontier areas for Christianity. The first student we sent out for the summer went to work with Muslim refugees in Berlin, Germany. Mostly, he would be working alongside German pastors and an American missionary couple who were aiding Kurdish refugees. These refugees had few friends in Germany, and they had many needs—social, physical, and spiritual.

Our seminary student, whom I will call Chad, arrived after the American missionary couple had been working with Kurds for over a decade. They had helped many Kurds learn German, find housing, and get jobs, but there had been few opportunities to talk about the Christian faith or even to read the Bible. It just so happened that summer when Chad was working with the couple, a group of Kurdish leaders said to the missionary couple, "We want to have a meeting at your church to learn about what you do and why you do it." So the meeting was set up in the fellowship hall of the German church. A long table was set up so the Kurdish elders could sit at the table with the German pastor and the American missionaries. Above the table, on the wall was a picture of the Last Supper.

Light snacks were served, and there was much nervousness and indecision as to how to proceed. Unprovoked, but providentially, a young girl pointed to Judas in the Last Supper painting in the room and said, "Who is that man? He looks mean." The missionary couple took turns telling the story of Jesus and the Last Supper, ending with the betrayal by one of Jesus' closest friends.

Suddenly, one of the Kurdish elders stood up and said. "Ha, then Jesus understands us. We have also been betrayed by our friends. That is why we are refugees here in Germany, and many of our friends have been killed. Our own neighbors in Iraq betrayed us. Yes, Jesus would understand us. Tell us more about Jesus." And so a small Kurdish church began in Berlin. Out of their own suffering, they could understand the cruciform nature of God.

This cruciform apostolicity is in the very DNA of Christianity. The historian of Christianity should be fitted with glasses that can see these elements in Christian history, or see the opposite: where Christians have collapsed the gospel into a story of success and conquest. Thus, these lenses give us historical vision and discernment. Without the humility of the cruciform Christian existence (even the humiliation of suffering), Christianity is presented as a religion of success and often of pride and personal glory. Far too often in the West, it has been presented as the royal faith of kings and queens, of princesses and princes. There are many instances of Christianity being expressed in such a way, and in each case it is a misrepresentation of Jesus and of his followers. We merely need to mention such misrepresentations for the lesson to be learned. Here are a few:

- the work of the Jesuits in the Inquisition in Europe
- the Crusades, with Christian soldiers fighting against Muslims
- the White Afrikaner Church and its oppression of blacks and coloreds
- white churches that supported enslaving Africans and also supported the Ku Klux Klan
- all forms of "prosperity" Christianity that make promises of easy health and wealth

All of these, and far too many more, are examples of Christianity avoiding humility and suffering for others, which is essential to Christian existence. However, Christianity is not masochistic and melancholy but eschatological and hopeful. As we saw in the previous chapter, there is time, and time moves toward fulfillment. As we saw in this chapter, Scripture affirms that suffering is a path, not a goal. Suffering points to unending joy and glory, and it is to that we now turn in the next chapter.

Chapter Four

Glory: The Humility and Hope of Heaven

The one who knows the mystery of the cross and the tomb,
knows the reasons of things. The one who is initiated
into the infinite power of the Resurrection, knows the purpose
for which God knowingly created all.

MAXIMUS THE CONFESSOR

Heavenly-mindedness, then, turns up the volume on our moral register
so that we are more alert to the pains of our precious sisters and
brothers. . . . It frees us up to give up what is ours for the sake of others.

MICHAEL ALLEN

After this I looked, and there was a great multitude that no one
could count, from every nation, from all tribes and peoples and languages,
standing before the throne and before the Lamb. . . . They cried out
in a loud voice, saying, "Salvation belongs to our God who is seated on
the throne, and to the Lamb!" . . . For this reason they are before the throne
of God, and worship him day and night within his temple, and the one
who is seated on the throne will shelter them. They will hunger no more,
and thirst no more; the sun will not strike them, nor any scorching heat;
for the Lamb at the center of the throne will be their shepherd, and he will

> *guide them to springs of the water of life,*
> *and God will wipe away every tear from their eyes.*
>
> REVELATION 7:9-11, 15-17

W E STARTED THIS VOLUME talking about time. God is beyond time, but out of his great love he created time and populated his time-bound creation with his own image: people. Thus, as humans go through time, they think and act and feel. They also hope and dream. History emerges in this human development through time. In chapter three we looked at the center of all of history—Jesus. In the incarnation, life, death, resurrection, and ascension of Jesus we see revealed the deeper love of God, which points toward an eventual fulfillment of that love. That love was revealed in suffering for others, and that same love continues to be expressed in Christ's body, the church. Now we look at the end or goal of history, which is glory. Glory is one way of expressing this hope, but more to the point, we can talk about the kingdom of heaven. Heaven, where God reigns and sin and its effects are no more, is what this chapter is about.

As we talk about glory and the hope of heaven, we will see that this orientation makes sense of many other issues related to history and human life. We will talk about the need for a hope that is genuine and true. We will also see the connection between the hope of glory and both personal transformation and ethical behavior. We will see the relationship between Christian suffering and Christian hope. We will look at historical stories where we see this hope of glory being lived out in the lives of Christian leaders and institutions. Along the way we will try to make sense of *glory*, a term with many uses in the Bible and present parlance. Finally, we will see that false hopes, or false glory, tend toward ideologies that are destructive of human thriving. We start off with the relationship between chapters three and four, suffering and glory.

THE WAY AND THE DESTINATION

We now complete our trinity of key concepts for the study of Christian history: glory. Suffering by itself is hopeless, and we might even say that without Christ, it is not redemptive. It is not theologically responsible to end a discussion of Christian suffering with suffering itself. In Christian theology suffering must be related to both joy and glory. In the last chapter we looked at many of the verses in Scripture that point to the relationship between the sufferings of Jesus and the glory that was then revealed in his crucifixion, resurrection, and ascension. In all of these passages it is evident that suffering does not have purpose or value on its own. Suffering is a meaningful pathway to obedience and holiness, and eventually to glory.

But more than a pathway, Paul ends up talking about suffering as part of the paschal mystery. "I am now rejoicing in my sufferings for your sake, and in my flesh I am completing what is lacking in Christ's afflictions for the sake of his body, that is, the church. I became its servant according to God's commission that was given to me for you, to make the word of God fully known. . . . [This] mystery . . . is Christ in you, the hope of glory" (Col 1:24-25, 27). What does this mean except that his suffering is mystically bound up in the sufferings of Jesus Christ which we remember each time we celebrate the "mysteries" (*sacramentum*). It is not just an individualistic occurrence but a part of our being in community as the body of Christ. Paul's suffering is "for your sake" and "for the sake of his body, that is, the church."

As we noted in the last chapter, I believe one of the key passages that makes the connection of suffering and glory so clear and so clearly Christological is found in 1 Peter. This letter of Peter was written to people who were suffering as exiles or migrants. They had experienced persecution and were, therefore, suffering for their faith in Jesus. Peter reminds them of the value of their salvation (more precious than gold) and then identifies their suffering with the very identity of Jesus.

> Concerning this salvation, the prophets who prophesied of the grace that was to be yours made careful search and inquiry, inquiring about the person or time that the Spirit of Christ within them indicated when it testified in advance to the sufferings destined for Christ and the subsequent glory. It was revealed to them that they were serving not themselves but you, in regard to the things that have now been announced to you through those who brought you good news by the Holy Spirit sent from heaven—things into which angels long to look! (1 Pet 1:10-12)

Later in the letter he makes it clear that Jesus' predicted suffering and glory is also part of the life of those who are "in Christ." "Sharing in Christ's sufferings" gives a whole new depth of meaning to their difficult circumstances. "This is not just a difficult time; this is part of your identify in Jesus Christ" is what Peter is saying.

> Beloved, do not be surprised at the fiery ordeal that is taking place among you to test you, as though something strange were happening to you. But rejoice insofar as you are sharing Christ's sufferings, so that you may also be glad and shout for joy when his glory is revealed. If you are reviled for the name of Christ, you are blessed, because the spirit of glory, which is the Spirit of God, is resting on you. (1 Pet 4:12-14)

There are many passages of Paul that identify the relationship between suffering and glory. Particularly, for Paul, the central concern about suffering is as it relates to the suffering of the missionary for other people. Paul talks about suffering that occurs *so that* others will hear the good news.

> Although I am the very least of all the saints, this grace was given to me to bring to the Gentiles the news of the boundless riches of Christ, and to make everyone see what is the plan of the mystery hidden for ages in God who created all things; so that through the church the wisdom of God in its rich variety might now be made known to the rulers and authorities in

the heavenly places. This was in accordance with the eternal purpose that he has carried out in Christ Jesus our Lord, in whom we have access to God in boldness and confidence through faith in him. I pray therefore that you may not lose heart over my sufferings for you; they are your glory. (Eph 3:8-13)

And of course when it comes to suffering, one of the key questions is simply, Is it worth it? This suffering seems to be too much—the loss of health, the loss of freedom, the loss of loved ones. Is it really worth it, or is it all vanity? Both Paul and Peter answer with a resounding and clear response.

For you did not receive a spirit of slavery to fall back into fear, but you have received a spirit of adoption. When we cry, "Abba! Father!" it is that very Spirit bearing witness with our spirit that we are children of God, and if children, then heirs, heirs of God and joint heirs with Christ—if, in fact, we suffer with him so that we may also be glorified with him. I consider that the sufferings of this present time are not worth comparing with the glory about to be revealed to us. For the creation waits with eager longing for the revealing of the children of God. (Rom 8:15-19)

There are many other verses expressing the same concept in longer passages and in parables. Any Christian theology of suffering will also be inseparable from a theology of hope, glory, and joy. The theological taproot of the gospel is that suffering and death do not have the last word. Jesus is the icon of suffering for us. Suffering is the path or the way to glory. This way of suffering is temporary, and it has its own severe gifts for us, such as humility and self-awareness. And while the way is temporary, the destination is eternal. Glory is endless.

Of course, there is suffering in this life, and then there is also *sacred* suffering. Humans suffer just by being human.[1] The suffering we have

---

[1] Jordan B. Peterson writes about the suffering that comes to all humans as an opportunity for developing character. Thus, even on a very human and secular level (Peterson is not a religious believer), suffering can be a path to the Good. "Life is suffering. That's clear. There is no more basic, irrefutable truth." *12 Rules for Life: An Antidote to Chaos* (Toronto: Random House, 2018), 161.

been talking about in this volume is not what is common to all but what is sacred or special to the Christian life, either on the path to faith or as part of the life of faith. It is related to Jesus' clear teaching that "unless a kernel of wheat falls to the ground and dies, it remains only a single seed. But if it dies, it produces many seeds" (Jn 12:24 NIV). Similar teachings are found throughout Jesus' discourses: "Whoever wants to be my disciple must deny themselves and take up their cross and follow me" (Mt 16:24 NIV). This type of sacred suffering is the result of true discipleship, identification with Jesus even in his suffering and death. "Set your minds on things above, not on earthly things. For you died, and your life is now hidden with Christ in God. When Christ, who is your life, appears, then you also will appear with him in glory" (Col 3:2-4 NIV). Such suffering and death is redemptive because it ends in glory. So, we can envision and receive suffering and death as the gateway to glory. The two are of one life, lived in the one true life, which is now in glory.

THE MEANING OF GLORY

But what is glory? Few words are more complex and nuanced but also as important to Christian identity and thought than the word *glory*. We cannot simply look at the etymology or original meanings of the Hebrew (*kavod*) and Greek (*doxa*) words to understand what the English, French (*glorie*), German (*der Ruhm* or *die Herrlichkeit*), or Chinese (*Róngyào*) words actually mean.

Both the Hebrew and Greek words used for what we translate as glory are used in a variety of ways. One way the word is used is of human glory, such as praising a person for their work or works. But this glory is generally a way of describing human pride or self-adulation. It is as if we are robbing the glorious one of his glory. It is therefore negative.

Glory throughout Scripture is mostly used of God: God's nature, character, reputation, presence, or the honor he is due. This is how we are using the word here. Before describing just how important it is for the understanding of Christian history, let's look more closely at the various facets of this word.

Glory is used throughout the Bible as a summary of the presence of God. God's presence is often described as radiating light and creating fear. God's glory is observable, as when Moses went up the mountain to be with YHWH and "to the Israelites the glory of the LORD looked like a consuming fire on top of the mountain" (Ex 24:17 NIV). When the divine glory of Jesus was revealed in the transfiguration, we read that "the appearance of his face changed, and his clothes became as bright as a flash of lightning." When Peter, James, and John "became fully awake, they saw his glory and the two men standing with him" (Lk 9:29, 32 NIV). So glory has a physical manifestation: it will shine as brightness.

God's glory also is full of power. Humans, when confronted with the glory of God's presence, are often filled with fear; they fall face down in worship. "Moses and Aaron went from the assembly to the entrance to the tent of meeting and fell facedown, and the glory of the LORD appeared to them" (Num 20:6 NIV). "When all the Israelites saw the fire coming down and the glory of the LORD above the temple, they knelt on the pavement with their faces to the ground, and they worshiped and gave thanks to the LORD, saying, 'He is good; his love endures forever'" (2 Chron 7:3 NIV). Divine presence is overwhelming in power, light, and life. It is not possible to remain self-confident or self-absorbed in the presence of God's glory. However, the cause of fear in the presence of God's glory is that his glory is holy and pure, whereas we are sinful and therefore judged by his very presence. The author of Hebrews, when summarizing the first appearance of God's glory at the reception of the Ten Commandments, ends with this little phrase: "Our God is a consuming fire" (Heb 12:29, quoting Deut 4:24).

Glory, as we learn mostly in the Psalms, points to God: his nature, his law, his will, his power, his holiness, his judgment, his salvation, even his beauty (Ps 27:4). Thus, God's glory is the reflection of all that God is and all that he has done and will do. God's glory is not a general glow or mist, even though at times it comes as a cloud or a fire. God's glory is apocalyptic, meaning that it reveals his character and work. Thus, glory has real meaning that is observable (according to his law), and it has meaning that is deeper than humans can ever plumb and higher than humans can scale. When Jesus raised Lazarus from the dead, some of the saving power of God's glory was seen. When Jesus healed the woman who had been bleeding for twelve years, something of the healing glory of God was observed. In turning over the tables of the money changers in the temple, the glory of God's justice was being revealed. We can say this is the nature, reputation, judgment, and love of God being seen in the life of Jesus.

God's glory is also seen in his creation. In fact, many theologians talk about the two ways God, and therefore his glory, is revealed to humanity: general revelation (creation) and special revelation (Scripture, miracles, and Jesus). Creation is an imperfect depiction of God's glory because of its destructive outbursts, and yet it does point to the greater glory of the one who is glorious. The vastness of oceans and mountain ranges; the complex structures of plant, animal, and human life; the remarkable beauty of sunsets and coral reefs; and the power of hurricanes all point to the God who brought all of this into being. God's glory is seen in creation, and therefore our treatment of his creation says something about our honor or worship of God. It is easy to see why people throughout history have been tempted to worship creation (sun, stars, mountains) instead of the Creator. Creation is worthy of our artwork, our poetry and study. God is worthy of much more: worship.

For the sake of this study, we need to talk about two types of glory: in and out of time. There is the *future glory*, where all is glorious and full of love: heaven. Peter talks about this future hope in the following manner: "By his great mercy he has given us a new birth into a living hope through the resurrection of Jesus Christ from the dead, and into an inheritance that is imperishable, undefiled, and unfading, kept in heaven for you, who are being protected by the power of God through faith for a salvation ready to be revealed in the last time" (1 Pet 1:3-5). It is this future hope of glory that guides our life in the present. Future glory is our present guidance. It is this future glory of heaven that orients our present existence. This future and eternal glory is what drives Christian history and what makes the second type of glory exist.

The second type of glory is seen in the life and work of Christians and their churches throughout history. These "little glories" are signposts that point to eternal glory. If heaven is a place of no more tears (Rev 7:17), then the work of Christians to take away tears are little glories pointing to heaven. If heaven is a place where every tongue and tribe and people and nation is represented (Rev 7:9), then instances of including all languages and nations are little glories pointing to heaven. If the eternal glory will be a place where God is everywhere radiating his glorious light, then any places and times where the truth and brightness of God are brought into dark places are little glories. If heaven is a place of love and justice, then times and places where injustices are ended and love reigns are signposts of the greater glory. The goal circumscribes the life and work of the Christian.

Thus, as the church expresses the glory of God—obeying his commandments, living into Christian virtues, and living for others—more of God's glory is approximated in time in specific times and places. Little glories become evidence of the church's discipleship in this world in time. Another way of expressing this is that we are talking about glory in two dimensions, both as the "not yet" future hope and the "now" as partially revealed in the life and work of the church.

First, as for the future hope, we are talking about glory eschatologically, or the really real future. Glory used in this way is the new heavens and the new earth where God is in residence, and there is no need for the sun. This is the glory where there will no longer be scorching heat, lack of water, or tears (Rev 7:16-17). In this case all that we have said about glory will have become reality: the light, righteousness, holiness, peace, and absolute love and beauty. American theologian Jonathan Edwards tried to express the heavenly reality as the full expression of God's love in a sermon titled "Heaven Is a World of Love" (1749). It is this full love of God expressed as glory that propels time forward and is the focus of the church, propelling her forward in good works and missionary outreach. This glory is both our foundation for worship and our motivation in mission.

Second, we are using glory here as the "now" of the kingdom of God, not yet fully revealed but seen as in a mirror darkly on earth. Jesus has initiated the coming kingdom, and we see some of its lines. These shadows and mists of glory are a foretaste of the heavenly kingdom. What are these little glories? When we see the homeless being housed and fed, or when we see the illiterate learning to read and then becoming gainfully employed, we are seeing a little of what the heavenly realm will be like. It is these little revelations of the kingdom of heaven that show the true glory of God's law and Jesus' life and teachings. When we see these little glories coming about through the sacrifice and faithfulness of the church, others might say, "It is true, when we do not covet, when we do not lie, and so on, something glorious happens." The kingdom begins to be revealed as Jesus is honored, and his Word penetrates the lives of his own and spills out to transformed lives and cultures.

GLORY, HOPE, AND THE HOPE OF GLORY

The reality of future glory and the signs of that glory in this world both give hope to Christians. Knowing that one's sin has been forgiven and that Jesus has gone to prepare a place for you gives one hope even when the signs around are not very positive. This is true for the Christian, and it goes a long way in describing the type of sacrifices Christians make to serve others and see others come to faith. But these signs of little glory now and the teachings of sin being forgiven and death being conquered also give hope to those outside of the church. Both words and works are signs and symbols for the outsider. Many come to faith when they see the faith enacted and hear it interpreted. Jesus' words are explanations of his works, and his works are illustrations of his teachings. The same is true for the Christian whose life is in Christ. Her or his life points to future glory, and therefore it gives hope.

People without hope become despondent, lethargic, and inactive. People with hope have reason to act, respond, and change. Hope motivates and directs. Hope motivates people to resist their own oppressions and to struggle for others. In other words, hope does not just have a personal power or motivation, but it serves others. Hope has both a communal as well as an outside dimension. The hope of glory motivates a person to serve and even suffer for others so that their story can be included in the heavenly story.

It is helpful to state clearly that hope and the glorious vision of heaven has motivated missionary activity in the church throughout its history. The times when there was little missionary activity in the church must be seen as the exception. From the very earliest years after the ascension of Christ, it was the forgiveness of sins and hope of heaven, coupled with the commission from the risen Lord, that propelled Christians in mission. We often think about this only in terms of the early Roman Empire and then imperial missions in the West, but it was also true from the very beginning in Africa and Asia.[2]

---

[2]See Scott W. Sunquist, "Ancient Christianity in Asia" and "Asian Theological Education: Earliest Trajectories," chaps. 2 and 15 in *Explorations in Asian Christianity: History, Theology and Mission* (Downers Grove, IL: IVP Academic, 2017). See also Vince Bantu, *A Multitude of All Peoples: Engaging Ancient Christianity's Global Identity* (Downers Grove, IL: IVP Academic, 2020).

The earliest Syrian and Persian Christians moved out in mission across the Persian frontier to India and eventually to China to proclaim the good news and to establish churches and bishoprics. And Christians, driven by this hope, moved across North Africa as well as down the coast of East Africa carrying the same message and establishing communities built around the same teachings of hope from a God who is alive and invites all into his kingdom.

In the past we may have said the motivating factor was obedience to Jesus' final command. God said "Go," and so Christians went out in mission. And that, of course, is part of the truth. But we know that the Great Commission was not a motivating verse or concept for mission (with the exception of St. Patrick) until well after the Reformation.[3] It was not the main motivating force for many except for Protestants in the end of the nineteenth century up to the present time. Christians have mostly been moved to spread the faith because of what has happened in their life, the promise of forgiveness and eternal life, and the evidence seen in lives and cultures changed. The greater glory (eschatology) as well as little glories drive mission.[4] The future pulls us forward in the present.

This hope not only drives mission and generates transformation, but eschatology and hope also shape ethical decisions. Many theologians and ethicists have made this connection: ends drive both means and decisions in the present. John Howard Yoder understood glory as an ethical spirituality. As he said it, our ethical spiritually means

---

[3]Justinian von Welz, in 1664, may have been the first to refer to Matthew 28 as the Great Commission, but it was not commonly used by Protestants until the nineteenth century. See Wolfgang Bruel, "Theological Tenets and Motives of Mission: August Hermann Francke, Nikolaus Ludwig von Zinzendorf," in *Migration and Religion: Christian Transatlantic Missions, Islamic Migration to Germany*, ed. Barbara Becker-Cantarino (Amsterdam: Rodopi, 2012), 41-60.

[4]Jurgen Möltmann is one of the strongest proponents of the role of eschatology in mission. And, more to the point for this volume, he links eschatology with suffering and the apostolic nature of the church. See Scott Sunquist, *Understanding Christian Mission: Participation in Suffering and Glory* (Grand Rapids, MI: Baker Academic, 2013), 277-78. See also Andrew Walls, "Eschatology and the Western Missionary Movement," *Studies in World Christianity* 27, no. 1 (2016): 182-200; Oscar Cullmann, "Eschatology and Missions in the New Testament," in *The Theology of Christian Mission*, ed. Gerald Anderson (New York: McGraw-Hill, 1961), 42-54.

we "live in the world as a sign of divine presence." This is to then see "history doxologically."[5] Thus, the intentional missionary work and ethical decisions we make are shaped by eschatological hope, the hope of glory as we express it here.

SOME STORIES: LIVES IN TIME, SUFFERING TOWARD GLORY

To give some life or reality to these ideas we now turn to history. How do we see this hope of glory driving mission and ethical decisions in such a way that Christians will accept suffering and loss as well as extreme personal deprivations? Let me introduce a story or two to show how this framework guides our reading of Christian history. The church in China is my first illustration. Christianity has been introduced five times in China, four times by West Asians or Europeans and the fifth time internally by persecuted, displaced, and oppressed Christians. The oppression that Christians received under the late Tang Dynasty (including the transition to the Song Dynasty), the persecutions under the Yuan, then under the Qing, and finally under the Communists would lead any historian to see China as hopeless for Christianity. In fact, when I was in graduate school we spoke almost in an embarrassed way about the great expense and sacrifice that was made to bring Christianity and its benefits to China. Many Western missionaries sacrificed to bring a religion the Chinese did not want to an ancient culture that was difficult to penetrate. Disease, violence, suspicions of foreign imperial oppression, and collusion with opium traders all seemed to compromise the message. When "liberation" came in 1949, very few people were optimistic; the progressive social program of Christianity would now be promoted by a government that also was socialist. There was a brief period of hope after years of oppression by Japanese imperialism and then ongoing civil war.

---

[5] I owe these insights from Yoder to J. Alexander Sider, *To See History Doxologically: History and Holiness in John Howard Yoder's Ecclesiology* (Grand Rapids, MI: Eerdmans, 2011), 4.

Such hope—that a government could be seen as the fulfillment of Christian hopes—was another incarnation of imperial Christianity. The motto "Love the country, love the church" has been a general aspiration expressed by Chinese Christians in the China Christian Council. Of course, such a sentiment can be viewed as a healthy expression when we look at the difficult history of Christianity in China. But it has a different ring when a Klansman from Tennessee says it than when a bishop or church official from China says it. Still, it has the same genetic flaw. Any hope that we have for the church in conflating love of country and church, or in seeing the government fulfilling some of the vision of the church, is misplaced hope. In recent history we can express our gratitude when the Chinese government returns properties, allows Bibles to be printed, or actually builds churches at government expense (which it has done). We are also grateful when the Singapore government builds Christian ("mission") schools or pays the salaries of Christians who are running Christian drug rehab homes. We should be grateful for "faith-based" government-supported initiatives. However, the hope of the gospel and the revelation of Jesus for the nations are found in none of these. To put our hope in such arrangements is idolatry. To accept such help is to express gratitude.

China, however, has another lesson for us. After four advances and then a sudden generation-long period of oppression (churches closed, church leaders sent off to camps, missionaries expelled, etc.), Christianity was finally "translated" into Chinese culture.[6] Christianity entered Chinese culture and began to make its home there. From a foreign religion, it came to be expressed as a Chinese religion. From a foreign-supported faith, it became a self-supporting shoot of a plant. What missionaries and mission societies attempted for centuries was unwittingly accomplished through the generation of suffering brought

---

[6]For a presentation of the four advances of Christianity in Asia see Sunquist, *Explorations in Asian Christianity*, 11-26.

on by Mao Zedong. The numerous periods of suffering have brought the present period of glory for the church in China. Many scholars of Chinese religions (and specifically of Chinese Christianity) have quietly predicted that the amazing explosion of Christianity in China is still before us. There is still great interest among the Chinese in learning about Christianity, and Chinese Christians continue to be zealous in both missionary outreach and in personal evangelism. It is not only that growth will continue in China, but cruciform apostolicity will be expressed as more Chinese will look for pathways for mission outreach.

But we must remember that this future glory, which may or may not come in our lifetime, has been sown in suffering. Another story will illustrate my point that Christian mission is always sown in suffering and always points to the future glory of God for the nations. At the 2007 bicentennial celebration of the arrival of the first Protestant missionary to China, Robert Morrison, I was approached by two different Chinese scholars, one from Wuhan and one from Shanghai, telling me that they have discovered that the modern terms the Chinese have for mathematics and physics were developed by Christian missionaries. They thought I would be interested to learn this. For them it was a discovery; for me it was historical evidence.

Calvin Wilson Mateer, a graduate of the Pittsburgh Theological Seminary, where I was teaching at the time, encountered violence before and during the Boxer Rebellion in Shandong Province. He and his wife, Julia, were nearly broken during ongoing famines. Writing in his journal April 9, 1889, he recorded, "It is the hardest work I ever did in my life. To look all day long on a continual succession of starving people, and to be beset by their entreaties to enroll more names than you can, is very hard on the nerves. There is no end to the starving people."[7]

---

[7]Daniel W. Fisher, *Calvin Wilson Mateer: Forty-Five Years as a Missionary in Shantung, China; A Biography* (Philadelphia: Westminster, 1911), 289.

Earlier, upon arrival in China, Julia contracted cholera and nearly died. Her life was permanently impaired. Married in December 1862, she and Calvin traveled by train from western Pennsylvania to New York. They passed Gettysburg and one of Calvin's family homes by train as the troops were preparing for battle. Sailing out of New York, the missionaries were on watch for Confederate battle ships. It could be argued that in times of war, missionaries should stay at home and be peacemakers. And yet the Mateers went to a land where they were not wanted and proclaimed a belief that was considered foreign. They also went to a nation that was at war; a far worse war than the American Civil War. This was the time of the Taiping Rebellion, where nearly thirty million people would be killed. Childless, Julia spent her first nine and a half years mostly alone as her husband tried to exercise a gift he did not have: evangelism. After nearly a decade of itinerancy, Calvin returned home to find out that Julia's little school for boys had become a popular local institution to which poor local farmers would pay to send their sons. Julia had begun translating books into Chinese so young, rural, poor Chinese boys could study the best of modern knowledge.

This "little boarding school for boys" was highly effective. In 1895 it was considered the best educational institution in China. Of the forty-seven graduates in 1894, ten had studied for the ministry, and eleven were college professors. Others were teachers and lay leaders. When the University of Peking was started by the young emperor, who was aided by educational missionary W. A. P. Martin in 1897, twelve of the professors were Mateer graduates. The school was very effective in raising up faithful leaders for the church and for China. Now what was Julia's crosscultural educational theory? In the 1914 Mission Report from Shandong and in Julia's biography, we read of the following three principles:

1. Education *must be Christian,* "powerfully and effectively."[8]

2. Education *must be thorough* because this is the first quality of character building. We might add that building character was the central concern that Julia had in her work.

3. It *must be Chinese,* that is, fit for Chinese in their everyday life.

The curriculum was mostly what they knew from America, but they designed it for what would be best for China and for Chinese Christians. Thus, they substituted the Chinese classics for Greek and Latin. It is hard to imagine spending years learning the Chinese language and Confucianism and then teaching Confucianism to Chinese boys. In fact, they taught every course in Chinese. What that meant is that every textbook had to be written in Chinese. They were not in China to make Chinese think and speak English. Between the two of them they wrote the first Chinese book on how to read and sing Western music, the first books in Chinese on chemistry, mathematics, and physics, and the first book in Chinese on doing mental math. Julia's book on music—*The Laws of Western Music for Beginners with Songs Set to Music*—was the standard, written in 1872, and a third edition was published in 1907. Like the school itself, the music book was to help laity sing hymns and learn music theory. It was not to train professional musicians. The Mateers had no interest in training professionals. The focus was on teaching Chinese in their context to know their language and their culture, and to follow Christ with diligence in that context.

Two points regarding her educational theory ought to be noted, one on the Chinese context and one on imposing Western values. Julia learned and then either taught or had taught the Chinese classics of Confucius and Mencius for all of her students. Thus, they were learning the Chinese curriculum and adding much of the Western

---

[8]Robert M. Mateer, *Character-Building in China: The Life-Story of Julia Brown Mateer* (New York: Revell, 1912), 10.

curriculum. I have not found her saying more than a few words about
why she did this; she merely mentions that Greek and Latin were re-
placed with the more appropriate Confucian Classics in the curriculum. She believed that education must include cultural awareness
and appreciation. At the same time as she affirmed the culture, she
resisted another element of the culture. Chinese were taught the
classics by rote; they were literally to be able to repeat back the exact
Chinese characters. Julia introduced understanding, debate, and oral
presentations. All of this is very Western, and it comes in conflict with
Confucian models of learning and ordering society. She would spend
evenings visiting the boys in their rooms and asking them questions.
She introduced writing compositions and debating, where students
would prepare debates on subjects like the following:

- Which is more difficult, to rule by reason or by force?

- Which is better for this life, Christianity or Confucianism?

- Is it beneficial to be reviled?

- Which is better, to worship false gods or no god at all?

She taught young Chinese boys to think and reason and understand. Saturday mornings were times for "oration, essays, and dec-
lamations"—more oral practice. She even formed a literary society
to encourage reading and discussion of ideas. She wanted them to
be able to explain and defend their faith, and soon the whole school
was filled with Chinese Christian boys. As she expressed it, "In our
school the tongue is loosed, the thoughts are trained to come quickly
and to be expressed accurately."[9] With such high standards, and
combining some of the best of Chinese culture with the best that she
knew of Western education, Julia challenges Christians today
to think carefully about both the goals and methods of Christian
missionary work.

---

[9]Mateer, *Character-Building in China*, 45.

Julia brings us back to one of the questions at the beginning of this book, and that is what we make of social progress. But after the discussion of suffering in the last chapter, I believe we can now look at this differently. It is not the superiority of Christianity, or the great advances in science and technology, that brings progress in society. Julia was a broken and weak vessel who revealed the power of God in her weakness. Suffering is the prelude to glory. John Behr has written that Christian identity is found in the identity of Jesus Christ and his suffering.

> This divine grace is manifest when his betrayers, judges, and those who crucified him, turn to him (repent) to know him as their Savior. He is this because, as Peter affirms, following Isaiah, "when he suffered, he did not threaten" (1 Peter 2:23): in and through the sufferings we inflict, he does not condemn, resist, or exclude; he suffers violence, but never inflicts it—he is the lamb of God who bears the sin of the world (Jn 1:29). Such suffering is not merely passive—something forced upon Christ— but is voluntarily undertaken and, as such, is creative, making all things new (Rev 21:5).[10]

Christian identity is identity with the suffering Christ, and such suffering points to Christ's glory.

CHRISTIAN HISTORY IN SUFFERING AND GLORY

Not all missionaries are Julia Mateer, and not all Christians are happy with the idea of suffering. Most of us surely would prefer the more attractive way of power and glory. It seems very human to want to be safe, strong, and in control. But this is not the way of the Jesus movement. Our point here is that in our look at the history of Christianity, and in our acceptance of our lot as Christians today, we can look at the pattern of present suffering leading to eternal glory as normative. We can, therefore, critique Christians when they resort to

---

[10]John Behr, *The Mystery of Christ: Life in Death* (Crestwood, NY: St. Vladimir's Seminary Press, 2006), 75.

power or oppression to proclaim the suffering Messiah. And we can encourage those whose lot is temporary suffering. We have seen how Scripture describes this as the way of the cross.

Recovering a proper view of glory or the goal of missional existence is important today. This should take away the triumphalistic, colonial, or imperial nature of Christianity and replace it with a humble sense of divine glory that is costly. When Christianity is renewed or goes through a genuine revival, such humility and willingness to suffer for others (and to hope for glory) are evident.

A few years ago I attended an international and ecumenical conference on "revitalization movements." It was a three-day working conference. After listening to stories about robust revitalization movements from around the world that penetrate cultures, I came to a number of conclusions. Here is one of the conclusions from that conference: revitalization comes through deep personal repentance and drawing near to Jesus Christ, or it comes through an overwhelming concern for oppression or injustices. Whichever way it comes—we might say internally or externally—it eventually converts the other. If individual Christians are overcome by the treatment of women or children, it will humble them, and they will draw closer to Jesus Christ. If, however, they have a personal conversion to the suffering heart of Jesus Christ, they will turn to bear his burden for the poor and oppressed. We can think here of a Mother Teresa, St. Francis, St. Claire, the Moravians, Francis Xavier, or even Charles Finney, Robert Morrison, or Martin Luther King Jr.

One example will suffice. The Mulotins, or the Company of Mary, were started by Louis Marie de Montfort (1673–1716) in France. Louis Marie was moved by the social conditions of the time (external conversion). He wrote in 1701 concerning the church's condition and his calling: "When I see the needs of the Church, I cannot help but to plead continually for a small band of good priests ... under the banner and protection of the Blessed Virgin. . . . I feel a tremendous urge to make our Lord and his holy Mother loved, to go in a humble, simple way to teach catechism to the poor in country places and to arouse in sinners a devotion to our Blessed Lady and to go from parish to parish teaching catechism to the poor."

Montfort's small bands were a continuation of the seventeenth-century "missionary bands" that traveled around Europe for evangelistic and missionary purposes. St. Vincent de Paul's "Vincentians" were called the "Company of the Mission." Such bands revived local churches and called people to faithfulness regarding service to the poor and needy.

It is worth looking further at the ministry of the Mulotins or Company of Mary. This spirituality was in the tradition of the French school of spirituality, emphasizing a personal relationship with Jesus, but with a missionary calling. The actual ministry of the Mulotins involved a call to renewal of baptismal vows, religious processions through towns, and lively celebrative liturgies, all of which attracted the oppressed and poor but often raised the jealousy of local priests and bishops. When resistance came from local priests, Montfort carried his burden for his missions to Pope Clement XI, who affirmed his missionary calling and gave him the title of "Apostolic Missionary." The work of such diocese mission teams seems to have been quite effective. During the time of revolution and turmoil of the 1780s and 1790s in the area of Brittany, where Father Louis Marie worked, this region was among the most resistant to the Revolution. Among his most remembered and longest lasting contributions to the church are his hymns, poems, and devotional books, written to help the poor to both learn and to inculcate their faith.[11]

Christian vitality will always have these two elements impressed upon the heart: suffering on behalf of others in the pattern of Jesus Christ and the hope of glory for the world. As noted earlier, it is important to evaluate Christian missional movements through Scripture,

---

[11]See Dale T. Irvin and Scott W. Sunquist, *History of the World Christian Movement* (Maryknoll, NY: Orbis), 2:348-50.

the global Christian experience, and continuity with the founder, Jesus Christ. Similar patterns that reinforce this theme can be seen from ancient Christian writers. For example, Gregory of Nazianzus defended the truth of Christianity in this way: Christians do not fear death, so clearly they are living out the truth that death has been conquered. Thus, Christians do not fear suffering, for they know of the glory that has already been won.[12] Chrysostom and others agree. In the following passage, Chrysostom reminds the affluent and indulgent congregation that this world is not their home. There is a hope about which they need to be reminded.

> We do not live with the austerity that becomes Christians! On the contrary, we love to follow this voluptuous and dissolute and indolent life; therefore also it is but natural that we cleave to present things; since if we spent this life in fastings, vigils, and poverty of diet, cutting off all our extravagant desires; setting a restraint upon our pleasures; undergoing the toils of virtue; keeping the body under like Paul, and bringing it into subjection; not "making provision for the lusts of the flesh"; and pursuing the straight and narrow way, we should soon be earnestly desirous of future things, and eager to be delivered from our present labors.[13]

Most all monastic movements and healthy missionary movements were established with a similar mindset: the transitory nature of the present world, the call to alleviate sufferings and injustice, and the sure hope of eternal life in God's glory. Christian history is driven by such a spirituality of thought and life, which can be described by specific Christian fruits or virtues.

HOPE, HUMILITY, AND HOSPITALITY

There is a clear connection between cruciform apostolicity as a driving theme of Christianity and the hope of glory. This hope makes,

---

[12]Gregory of Nazianzus, *Oration 18* 42.

[13]John Chrysostom, *Homily VI* 7, in *The Nicene and Post-Nicene Fathers, First Series*, ed. Philip Schaff (Peabody, MA: Hendrickson, 2004), 9:384.

empowers, and guides the church to live for others, to die to self, and to work to see little glories in this world while keeping an eye on the next. Two more things need to be said before concluding. First, it is important to see the relationship between this suffering and glory and Christian virtues. Second, it is also important to take sin and evil seriously: What happens when there are false hopes replacing true divine glory? How does one understand this in reading Christian history?

One of the most fascinating recent studies of ancient Christianity was done by Alan Kreider, titled *The Patient Ferment of the Early Church*.[14] I believe it is an important book because it connects so carefully and thoroughly the Christian life and habits with the remarkable success of the early followers of Jesus in the Roman Empire. Kreider notes the common (and difficult to prove) explanations for how and why Christianity supplanted the well-embedded pagan and mystery religions of late antiquity. These common explanations (which I was taught in seminary) include the following:[15]

- in the clash of ideas, Christian ideas won out

- Christians' intolerant zeal

- teaching about the afterlife

- miraculous powers of Christians, including exorcisms

- austere morals

- organization of the church

- the Roman Empire's roads and communications

Kreider argues that these do not adequately or even accurately explain the unusual and rapid spread of Christianity throughout and beyond the Roman Empire. His explanation, argued carefully with ample evidence, is that Christianity spread rapidly because of four

---

[14]Alan Kreider, *The Patient Ferment of the Early Church: The Improbable Rise of Christianity in the Roman Empire* (Grand Rapids, MI: Baker Academic, 2016).

[15]Kreider, *Patient Ferment of the Early Church*, 1.

interrelated reasons: patience, *habitus*, catechesis, and ferment. For this section I want to focus on the first two and make brief comments about the last two.

Patience was not a significant virtue to the Greco-Roman cultures. In a sense this was a new value or approach to life for the ancients. It was key to the early Christians, for they understood clearly that God was patient with us, regarding our sin and his way of working out salvation, and that we should also be patient. Many early Christian treatises were written on patience. Christians showed their belief through the way they behaved, and they behaved with patience and forbearance.[16] In fact, the way they lived, the way they suffered, and the way they died showed that their faith in a loving God was expressed in a patient trust. Martyrdom stories are usually studied as stories of great faith and loyalty. But martyrdom accounts can also be studied as stories of patience and steadfastness.

Closely related to patience is *habitus,* or "reflexive bodily behavior" as Kreider defines it. What this means is that there is little indication that Christianity spread because Christians won arguments; in fact in the early church Christians were not as well-educated as many of their religious opponents. It took centuries before enough educated Christians could hold their own. Christianity did not spread by winsome rhetoric. Instead, "they grew because their habitual behavior (rooted in patience) was distinctive and intriguing. . . . When challenged about their ideas, Christians pointed to their actions. They believed that their habitus, their embodied behavior, was eloquent. Their behavior said what they believed; it was an enactment of their message."[17]

---

[16]Positive psychologists today have identified patience as one of two "instrumental virtues," meaning that along with self-control, these two make the expression of other virtues (love, generosity, gentleness, etc.) possible. See Sarah Schnitker, "An Examination of Patience and Well-Being," *Journal of Positive Psychology* 7, no. 4 (July 2012): 263-80. In the many psychological studies done now on virtues, it is clear that the New Testament and ancient Christians provide rich resources for the study of virtues, psychologically, philosophically, and ethically considered.

[17]Kreider, *Patient Ferment of the Early Church*, 2.

One of the habits that stood out in the first centuries was humility, which was often expressed as hospitality or care for the sick, even those outside the "family of faith." The supreme virtue for the early Christians was humility, expressed throughout Paul's letters (e.g., Phil 2:1-11; Eph 4:1-2; Col 3:12) and repeatedly by the ancient Christians.[18]

Since the earliest Christians met in homes, *habitus* was expressed mostly in house and table fellowship: hospitality. It was in close proximity that the *habitus* of Christians could be observed. Kreider mentions many practices or rhythms of life that would be counter-cultural and attractive, expressing the patience and humility that was at the core. These include the following "habits":[19]

- visiting the sick and prisoners
- putting money in the collection box for the poor
- eating together: table fellowship
- feeding needy people
- being truthful (and confessing/repenting when in error)
- maintaining sexual purity
- praising and thanking God at all times
- memorizing texts

Together these show the strong emphasis on the formation of lives in community that became interesting and then attractive to outsiders. And to connect with Kreider's third reason for the spread of Christianity, catechesis was important. People did not just "do ritual"; they were taught how to worship, how to think, how to live, and how to

---

[18]This is expressed throughout the early apologetic, martyrdom, and spiritual-theological litera-ture. John Cassian (d. 435) summarizes what was common knowledge in describing how to fight against the passions of the flesh: "The fathers also say that we cannot fully acquire the virtue of purity unless we have first acquired real humility of heart." *Philokalia*, trans. G. E. H. Palmer, Philip Sherrard, and Kallistos Ware (New York: Faber and Faber, 1979), 1:77.

[19]Kreider, *Patient Ferment of the Early Church*, 122-23.

relate to others. Formation was intentional, communal, and consistent. It was from this intentional and communal catechesis that the ferment developed.

What this reveals is that there is a close and integral relationship between suffering, glory, hope, ethics, mission, and virtues. This is very important for the study of Christian history. The trajectory of the church through time has been determined by the life of Jesus as lived in these interrelated themes. In the earliest church Jesus people were formed in such a way to be patient in the midst of suffering and to humbly wait for the Lord to act. Historically, we see these four themes of Kreider's woven through time and across the nations. It was the hope of glory that made such formation and patience both possible and necessary.

FALSE HOPES: IDEOLOGIES

As we have talked about glory, we have described it as the hope for the Christian and for the church. In other words, what is *really* real is what God has promised and shown in Jesus Christ. This was the reasoning of Gregory Nazianzen mentioned earlier. The kingdom of heaven will arrive, and when this happens, all of creation will be glorified in its worship of the Lamb. There will be no other worship and no other praise. All will be love and light. Everything else is decentered as God is the center of all, uniting all in perfect harmony through his love (Col 3:14).

Since this is the telos the church is pointing to, anything less is missing the mark (*hamartia*, "sin"). In the history of Christianity, we find many instances where Jesus is honored as a lord, as a cultural standard or moral teacher, but not as the eschatological Lord of all. When Jesus is dethroned, other authorities, meanings, or future hopes vie for first place. At times this is subtle, but at other times it is obvious. Slippery is the slope from Jesus being dethroned, to believing in another ultimate authority, to finding a new loyalty in an idol. We are created to worship, and when our worship is directed to anything less than God, the new object of worship is inadequate. Only worship of God can bear the weight of such glory. Humans are also predisposed to make ideas and assumptions about reality into new idols. These idols, when expressed as ideas about society, economic systems, or culture, become ideologies.

My point here is that false hopes that are not grounded in the life and work of God in this world are seedbeds for false worship and ideologies. In the post-Enlightenment, disenchanted West, false gods are usually ideologies. An ideology should be understood as the primary lens through which a person or a tribe or nation sees the world. It is the primary lens for interpreting events, people, and the world.

Three examples will help us understand this, two of which are more obvious and easier to accept. The third may be a little difficult for evangelical Christians. First, the Western progressivism of the nineteenth- and early twentieth-century Christians and empires was an ideology that often redirected Christians, especially those involved in mission, to trust too much in technology and governments. Progress was real. The early twentieth-century European or North American had a very different life from the early nineteenth-century human. Progress was seen in new forms of power, transportation, manufacturing, medicine, trade, and the newer social sciences. Western people knew more about other world religions in much greater detail than ever before. Western nations ruled most of the world. For Christians it was easy to (falsely) see this as God's method to help usher in the millennium. Millennial movements and mission movements inspired by progress came to center stage in Western Christianity. Christianity and progress were major themes of many Christian theologians and church leaders. As was mentioned in the beginning of this volume, James Dennis's three volumes of *Christian Missions and Social Progress* (1897–1906) is just one of many books and articles encouraging Christians to see the progress taking place because of the work of missionaries aided by technology, travel, and empires. To be honest, he was pointing out what we have called here little glories around the world that have come about because of missionary work.

However, the confidence, even hubris, that human (mostly secular) ingenuity was helping to bring about this "civilizing" was a major problem. A second major problem of interpretation was identifying "progress" with "civilizing" and identifying civilizing with looking like the West. Western clothes, Western-style music and worship, and even Western education and buildings were identified as the goal of civilizing. Some, but too few, could see the unholy collusion of Western progress with missionary endeavors. This was the missionary following the Jesus of power more than Jesus as the suffering servant. Not completely unrelated to this today are gospels of health and wealth and gospels of social influence (political leaders, Hollywood stars, etc.) built on false hopes.

Second, Marxism, along with Leninism, Stalinism, and Maoism, is a lethal substitute for a Christian eschatology that focuses on God's kingdom. Many people have written about Marxism as a secular substitute for Christian hope. Here I simply want to remind the reader that we have talked about how eschatology and the hope of a future is what drives people forward and shapes their lives. This has been a major theme of this book. People make decisions about life and death according to their eschatological hopes. However, ideologues, dictators, and narcissistic politicians use this knowledge of the potency of hope to leverage power. False hopes and dreams are often promoted by leaders, prophets, priests, presidents, and dictators. Often these hopes and dreams are very similar to the eschatology of the Bible without Jesus as the center.

In the case of Marxism and its cousins, the hope promised was given through a very specific view of history, a materialistic and deterministic one. The followers of Marx's historical teachings were merely pushing history forward a little faster; instead of an evolutionary change, they promised a revolution. The coming revolution was simply speeding up what would inevitably happen. Marxism is an ideology, and like all ideologies it not only tended toward oppression and violence; it created the largest death tolls, mostly intentional, of the twentieth century.[20]

Ideas matter, and shared ideas that bind people together in community matter the most. Some of the most destructive leaders in human history have been driven by a millennial or hopeful vision. Not only Marx but also Adolf Hitler had a vision of global harmony. Pol Pot in Cambodia had a vision for a future social order. Josef Stalin promised to bring a new secular order that would be egalitarian, but millions suffered under the false hope. In fact one of the major historical themes of the twentieth century was the rise of violent ideologies and related genocides. Genocide studies, developed in the final decades of the twentieth century agree that genocide is technically the attempt to eradicate a group of people (ethnic group, national group, religious group, etc.). Genocides are driven by ideologies, and they should be included in a listing of the violence of false hopes or secular eschatologies.[21] Not all false hopes and misplaced eschatologies end in mass killings and oppression, but all ideologies are false hopes that tend toward violence.

Finally, *dogmatic eschatologies* (especially strongly held ones) can also function as ideologies that drive Christian worship, mission, and even politics. In the past Christian mission was strongly supported by a postmillennial eschatology that basically taught that Jesus would return to earth after the thousand-year reign, which would be ushered

---

[20]It may not be the case that Mao intended to starve tens of millions of his own citizens in his Great Leap Forward, but that is what happened. He made misguided decisions based on bad history and an impossible future.

[21]See Israel W. Charney's *The Encyclopedia of Genocide*, 2 vols. (Santa Barbara, CA: ABC-CLIO, 1999).

in through the work of Christian mission (and social progress as mentioned above). All the nations will be reached, and the millennial reign will be initiated. This will be a period where most of the people of the world will be followers of Jesus, and righteousness will prevail in families, churches, and governments. After a thousand years of this peace, Jesus will return at the end of time and judge the world. Postmillennialism was the eschatology that led to much of the nineteenth-century missionary work and also much of the social reform and even the arguments against slavery. The social gospel movement was also indebted to this eschatology, a gradual and even organic growth of peace, Christian ethics, and morality. The power of such an eschatology can be seen in how Walter Rauschenbusch talked about this gradual development or progress while writing during the Great War. His lectures, delivered at the convocation of the Yale School of Religion in 1917, mentioned the War, but he still held on to a very optimistic millennial expectation. Still, this eschatology did bring about much work of social reform in the early twentieth century, as it did in the nineteenth century.

However, another eschatology began to develop in the nineteenth century, which has had very mixed results. This eschatology is expressed in the teachings of John Nelson Darby and codified and spread most widely through the iconic *Scofield Reference Bible*. Both Darby and C. I. Scofield were proponents of dispensationalism, a theology of time that marks God's work as having chapters or epochs where God works differently in his creation depending on the dispensation. Scofield had seven separate epochs, and leading up to the final age he taught that the Jewish nation of Israel would be reconstituted, the temple would be rebuilt, and sacrifices would once again occur in the temple. Thus, for the millions of fundamentalists who, in reading the Scofield Bible, have confused the Bible text with the notes, Israel and the temple are absolutely central. This has been taken as true dogma: Israel will become a nation, and Jesus will return on the Temple Mount.

Dispensationalism for many evangelical and fundamentalist Christians functions as an ideology. They vote for political leaders based on their support of Israel and the hope of the temple being rebuilt. Decisions about church, life, worship, and prayer are driven by this primary concern. There are even churches in many Asian countries that build prayer chapels specifically to gather Christians to pray for Jerusalem and for Jesus to return to a newly built temple in Jerusalem. Many of these groups plan pilgrimages to Jerusalem so they can pray on the land for the return of Jesus Christ. Many feel their mission for Jesus is about his return to Jerusalem more than their call to preach to the nations.

When we talk about the hope of glory, we have not talked in great detail about the second coming of Christ, neither the timing nor the elements that must be in place. The great teaching about the kingdom of heaven and the promise of God's "not yet" is what is important. Such detailed explanations that we find in dispensationalism are misleading and, for many people, their commitment to God's mission takes second place to an assumed future based on the nation of Israel. The result of this dogmatic presentation of last things has been an uncritical support of Israel among many evangelicals and fundamentalists as well as a reduction of Christians in the Middle East. The formation of Israel, support of the Jews, and disregard of the Palestinians has caused many Christians to emigrate from the Middle East.

The future eschatology or the future glory is what guides and motivates people, especially Christians. We have talked in this book about how that has worked out in history and how this must be a guiding principle in the study of Christianity in the past. History only has value as it instructs us and guides us. Such guidance comes only if we have a correct view of the teachings of Jesus, Christianity, the history of Christianity, and the hope of glory. We do better to focus on what Jesus asked us to focus on ("make disciples of all nations"), to live as he asked us to live (in all humility), to seek the things that are above (Col 3:1), and to remember we can trust him to be with us (Mt 28:20). This helps us to study history more helpfully and to live more faithfully.

Scottish theologian John Baillie, who once served as the president of the World Council of Churches, was known for investigating the knowledge of God and the spiritual, moral, and ethical life of the Christian. In 1936 he wrote a book of personal, and deeply theological, prayers (*A Diary of Private Prayer*).[22] It is only fitting that we close this chapter with a prayer that connects the issues of time and cross with the eternal glory that guides us forward in this life.

> O Eternal God, although I cannot see you with my eyes or touch you with my hands, give me today a clear conviction of your reality and power. Do not let me go into my work believing only in the world of sense and time, but give me grace to understand that the world I cannot see or touch is the most real world of all. My life today will be lived in time, but it will involve eternal issues. The needs of my body will shout out, but it is for the needs of my soul that I must care the most. My business will be with material things, but let me be aware of spiritual things behind them. Let me always keep in mind that the things that matter are not money or possessions, not houses or property, not bodily comforts or pleasures, but truth and honor and gentleness and helpfulness and a pure love of you. . . . On my pilgrim journey toward eternity, I come before you, the eternal One. Let me not try to deaden or destroy the desire for you that disturbs my heart. Let me rather give myself over to its persuasion and go where it leads me. Make me wise today to see all things within the dimension of eternity and make me brave to face all the changes in my life that come from this vision; through the grace of Christ my Savior.

---

[22]John Baillie, *A Diary of Private Prayer*, rev. Susanna Wright (New York: Scribner, 2014), 43.

Chapter Five

Faithful Reading of Christian History

RECENTLY I TAUGHT A COURSE on Asian Christianity. Most of the students were Asian or Asian American. The final paper was a research paper on an Asian Christian leader. My purpose in this assignment was to help the students see the importance of some of these early Asian Christian leaders and to show how Christianity develops differently in different contexts. After the papers were turned in, I had each student take ten to fifteen minutes to tell the rest of the class why we should know about their person. It was remarkable. Most of the students could have given an hour's impassioned lecture after completing their papers. They were excited about what they discovered. One student's presentation still stands out in my mind. She is a Chinese American, and she did her paper on the great Japanese Christian author, pastor, evangelist, labor organizer, and pacifist Kagawa Toyohiko (1888–1960). As she began to talk about his life chronologically, she quickly moved into a more impassioned mode: "And do you know what else he did?" Then she talked about his moving into the slum in Kobe, writing books and even novels to motivate others to care for the poor. And she concluded, "Why have I not heard of him before? He was so famous in his time, and his life was so Christian that he influenced many people. He had no division between bringing about social change and being an evangelist." By the time she was done, the class was motivated to learn from Kagawa.

My point is not that such hagiographical readings of history are good. Good history recognizes the shortcomings of all people, even our heroes of the faith. However, we need to allow history to teach us, to guide us, and to make us better people. There is no such thing as neutral or benign history. History at its core is about people, and so biography is the basic building block of story. We as people connect with people more than with institutions or movements. When we read biography, we read not merely as rational beings but as fully human beings with will, emotions, and mind entering into the human story.

There was a time, beginning with the Enlightenment, that it was thought that history was a matter of getting the facts right. If we got the facts right, we had an accurate history. Objectivity, facts, accuracy, and great people were the stuff of history. Of course this is still true, but that is not enough. As we have seen, history writing has gone through several transformations, especially in the past century. There are many lenses we can look through as we study history—psychological and sociological studies, power dynamics, gender studies, and so on. However, the argument here is that all of these are mere tools that may help to uncover motives or explain what has happened by focusing on causality. People act based on their own perceptions, habits, values, goals, hopes, and fears.

All of the various tools of historical analysis and scholarship must be used to make sense of Christian history as we have it here. Christian history is not neutral, but it is and must be written as a narrative that is pedagogical. Christian history, in all of its suffering and glory, must instruct us. If we do not allow it to instruct us, we have wasted our time on a pedantic and even frivolous activity. Merely studying events, documents, writings, sermons, and institutions without a lens or telos is often devoid of meaning. History *means* something; it has value as the retelling of a story of the past with both purpose and passion. I use the word *passion* intentionally, knowing that learning takes place when the mind and emotions are engaged. Good teaching does not neglect the emotions, but neither does good teaching misuse the emotions. Both rational thought and emotions can be manipulated. That is no reason to avoid using either the mind or heart in teaching and writing. My point is simply that at the end of the day, good historical writing is to be more than informative. It should also be transformative. There is value for individuals and society in the good and engaging writing and teaching of Christian history.

A simple illustration will illumine my point. For many people, especially school-aged children, the topic of history is boring. Biology, the study of dinosaurs, science fiction, and sports are engaging for young people. History? Few children say they love to study history. However, they may say they like to read biographies or short stories about people. Parents want children to read about heroes of the past. Today parents want to encourage their young daughters to read about famous women in history. If you ask someone why we study history, we usually get one of two answers. "I don't know why we study history. It's boring." Or, "I guess so we can learn from the past so we don't make the same mistakes." And that is the point. History should inspire us and humble us. History can make us better people.

The carefully researched study of Christian history has a purpose beyond merely knowing what happened. Embedded in every chapter, episode, and life are lessons for us, for our churches, and for society. This is closely related to, or is even an extension of, our study of the Bible. Christian history begins with creation, follows through the patriarchs, the early history of Israel, the teachings of the prophets, the incarnation and life of Jesus, the early missionary work of the apostles, and the writings of the apostolic fathers, and continues through the persecutions of the early church, the development of Christian empires, and the persecutions under other religious nations all the way up to last week's sermon or my morning devotions. Christian history is continuous. And, like the Bible itself, there are some sections that are more instructive and universally important than others. We should not feel guilty for valuing genealogical lists less than Psalm 23 or Matthew 11:28-30. The same is true of Christian history. Some people and events and writings are far more valuable and important and should be studied more carefully. Every event and life does not have the same value for us.

This book is about how to make these decisions understanding the essence of Christianity as a historical religion. We want to lift up and study the great examples of little glories that were brought about through much suffering. These are key themes to look for since Christian history points to the center of all of history.

READING HISTORY WITH THE POWER TO TRANSFORM

What else do we look for, and how else do we decide what to write about and what to read? Here is some historiographical guidance for young historians as well as for more seasoned historians to think about before writing or reading your next book on Christian history.

Read history looking for little glories. As we mentioned in the last chapter, little glories in this world point toward heaven and the hope we have in the consummation of all things in Jesus Christ. Thus when "tears are wiped away" and the nations come to faith through the work of intentional missionary work—when the hungry are fed and prisoners are visited—we see signposts of the kingdom. These we call little glories in contrast to the coming glory at the end of time. One of the important reasons for studying Christian history is to look for those little glories that come about through the church.

I believe this is one way that we help Christians "set your hearts on things that are above" (Col 3:1 NIV) as we reflect on how and why at certain times and places more of the kingdom broke into the view of all those around. Secular leaders notice when more of the poor are fed and housed through no work of their own. Such an inbreaking of the kingdom does not come without costs and suffering. For the homeless to be sheltered and people fed, we have to give up our own rights in order to serve others. People give sacrificially to help the poor knowing that sometimes these needy people may be taking advantage of them. However, the clear focus on Jesus' words, "Just as you did it to one of the least of these who are members of my family, you did it to me" (Mt 25:40), is what guides them in their sacrificial behavior.

We see these little glories in many places throughout the history of the church, but sometimes we have to look very closely and do detailed studies that look beyond official church records and the "great story" to see the little stories. Much of the sacrificial work that leads to little glories is done by neighbors, deacons, and widows and widowers, not by bishops, priests, and seminary presidents. This is the value of studying diaries of church members and the writings (letters) of missionaries. We see some of these little glories that were costly, but for us who follow later, they are great encouragements to faithfulness. I have found that in these stories of little glories produced at great cost, the persons who feature in them were people of great humility. This is why much detailed research is needed. These people, in all humility, counted others as more important than themselves. Such people do not advertise their work. They don't leave behind autobiographies about their important work. This leads us to the importance of biography.

Read history for biographies. History is not listing facts; it is narrative. It is story. Story is always about people, the decisions they make, and the forces that shape their options and directions. If life were entirely deterministic, this would not matter; but humans are free. They are not controlled by fate or external conditions.[1] We can

---

[1]The contrast here is with the pagan notion of fate as determined by birth and the heavens and is not intended to discount the Pauline understanding of predestination for good works (Rom 8:29) or for adoption (Eph 1:5). Humans are still free as created in the *imago Dei*.

choose how to respond and how to react even when our choices are limited. Therefore, in studying history we need to focus on biographies to understand how Christians are people "in Christ" seeking to live the life of Christ in particular contexts.

At times the local culture, with its restrictions, violence, and betrayal, seems to be too much, for the church and its leaders. And yet we see amazing resistance and renewal in some of the most difficult times. At other times, Christian leaders have all the opportunities and resources to grow and thrive, and instead they get caught up in the materialism and even the hedonism of the larger culture. This, along with the secularization of Western culture, is the story of Christianity in the West in the past century or so. How were Christian leaders making decisions that prevented them from pushing back against the incursion of the larger culture? Were they seduced by the power, influence, and wealth that was available? And conversely, who were the leaders who chose differently, and what evidence is there of their theology or motivation that we can pass on to others? Looking back at slavery in the United States and the decisions of Christian leaders, we can learn a lot about Christian courage, theology, ethics, community, and witness, especially in the South. Early martyrdom stories also are very instructive for the church ecumenical, for the early martyrs belong to all Christians. Studying the stories of Justin Martyr, Perpetua and Felicity, and the Persian martyrs under the Sasanian emperors is very instructive and inspirational.

Most Christians in the world talk about Christian saints. Icons are made to remind us of the ways these saints reflect Jesus Christ. There is something of Jesus in the lives of the saints. The idea is not just that we are to kiss the icon but that we take time to reflect and meditate on the lives of the saints. Protestants also have saints, but we usually call them missionary heroes. Others are great ecumenical leaders, preachers, evangelists (Billy Graham), or social reformers (Martin Luther King Jr.). It is important for the church to recover the idea of saints, heroes, or even prophets of the church. None of them was perfect, but we should encourage our congregations to be guided by those who have gone before us and have often suffered for their faithfulness to the gospel. This is not unsimilar to the way we study people in Scripture.

Read history for the influence of ideas (theology). I remember so well writing about the fifteenth century for *History of the World Christian Movement,* volume 2. I found it so amazing that the Chinese had built ships that traveled down the coast of Southeast Asia, across South Asia, all the way to the coast of East Africa long before the Portuguese made it down the coast of West Africa. The Chinese ships were three times the size of the ships of Columbus, which would not sail for another eighty-seven years. When I was doing this research and reading about the many trips of the Muslim Chinese admiral Zheng He (1371–1433) I thought to myself, *This is amazing! The Chinese, with the right ideas, could have conquered the world. They were far ahead of the little countries of Portugal and Spain.* But they didn't. Soon after these voyages, China once again turned back to itself and closed out the world. Work on the Great Wall expanded to keep out the world. The Chinese were the "Middle Kingdom," uniting heaven and earth, and they had no need for anything that Africa or South Asia had to offer.

Ideas matter. Theological ideas matter a lot. The struggles that the church has had over definitions of the Trinity and of the person of Jesus Christ are important. We behave differently and work differently when we see Jesus as a role model versus the Savior of the world and God incarnate. It matters also that the mission of God in the world is about human and cultural transformation and not just about making nice people nicer. It matters that we understand not only the depth of sin but also the power of God to bring about transformation.

However, many of the divisions of the church and arguments over finer points of doctrine are more divisive and destructive of Christian witness than reflective of God's will for his church. Our finite minds must accept the limits of our understanding of and ability to explain God and his ways. It is important to see the centrality of the Eucharist as pointing to Jesus and his suffering on behalf of humanity. This keeps us both focused and humble. We are rightly placed before God when we, on our knees (at least figuratively), receive his body and blood. Exactly how God is present in the Eucharist (or whether it should be called the Lord's Supper) is less important than that we remember, celebrate, repent, and receive his body for us.

And what about eschatology? Is there one way of expressing what will happen when Jesus himself even said, "But about that day and hour no one knows, neither the angels of heaven, nor the Son, but only the Father" (Mt 24:36)? It is important to know what we must know, what we can know, and what we must pass on to others. It is equally important to have the humility to know what we cannot know and must not pass on as necessary. In the study of Christian history we have far too many instances of Christians dividing over unnecessary and unknowable doctrines. The history of Protestantism and Pentecostalism is overflowing with unnecessary divisions and arguments over nonessential doctrines. It takes both humility and wisdom to step away from such entanglements in fruitless arguments that distract the church from what is necessary and central. Ideas matter. It also matters that we know what ideas matter, what are inconsequential, and what we cannot fully know as we see through a glass darkly (1 Cor 13:12).

Read history for our local churches. Christian history is taught in seminaries so future pastors and other church leaders will know about their own history (why we believe what we do about the Eucharist, etc.) and will be able to maintain their particular tradition. However, until recently a great deal of church history was really about maintaining distinctions and divisions. There were church history books written by Dutch Reformed historians that were very different from Kurt Aland's very Lutheran *History of Christianity*, which is very different from Roman Catholic church history books. Such sectarian histories are less and less significant in the twenty-first century. There is still the need to tell a history that explains why we do what we do (as Presbyterians or Orthodox) and to explain what we believe. The four major families of Christianity will not go away, even if the differences within these major families shift and recede.[2]

Of greater significance on the other side of Western Christendom is to study the meaning of Christian communities in largely non-Christian contexts. Today virtually no Christians live in a Christendom context. Governments, media, technology, and social systems are at best neutral and often opposed to Christianity or specific teachings of the church. The study of Christian history now takes on a new meaning and significance. Local church leaders and their congregations need to understand better how the church has lived as a minority or as a community under persecution. Often the church has been seduced or gently persuaded by governments or the media to deny some of its basic teachings. Awareness of these past scenarios will help Christians today be attentive to the little compromises that are acceptable and the ones that that are not.[3] This newer focus in our historical study should lead us to de-emphasize differences between Christian families and within Christian families. The big differences that should grab our attention now are the differences between the church and larger society. How is the church, even our local church, influencing the local culture, or how is it being led along by the local culture?

Read history to meditate on the ambiguities of history. So much of Christian history is filled with ambiguities. Why do good people

---

[2]Roman Catholic, Orthodox, Protestant, and Spiritual. This designation goes back to the early days of the World Council of Churches and the writings of Lesslie Newbigin. See *The Household of God: Lectures on the Nature of the Church* (London: SCM Press, 1957). Newbigin's divisions are determined by how authority is defined in each church family.

[3]Recently some churches in the United States have taken their stand that the government cannot tell them they must close and go to worship online. Other churches see this (not having corporate worship) as a small compromise for the health of others.

doing the work of the kingdom suffer as they do? How can a church do so much good and then be so racist? How can followers of the Prince of Peace be so violent and warlike? I remember teaching about Origen in my first year in Singapore, and after a carefully thought out lecture a student raised his hand and asked simply, "Professor, was Origen a Christian or not?" Well, Origen was a complex historical figure. The story of Origen's self-castration, his doctrine of the pre-existence of souls, and his teaching that all will be saved (universalism) are troubling to most of us. And yet overall his writings were orthodox, and he was one of the first systematic theologians to defend the Christian faith.

One of the major ambiguities in Christian history is the nearly fifteen hundred years of Christendom in various forms. Jesus did not teach that we are to try to convert nations-states but people and peoples. The Greek word is *ethne*, which would be more like an ethnic group, not a modern nation. Political entities like a nation-state or an empire throughout history have claimed to be Christian, even with a "state church." When this happens we have a very ambiguous blessing. Often Christian-influenced laws are passed, and Christian values guide much of the political culture. The nation can respond to crises with humility, repentance, lament, and even worship. This is wonderful when Christian rulers lead the people in such Christian virtues as humility and generosity and even care for the poor.[4]

However, what does it mean for a Christian nation to declare war on another Christian nation? Where is the theme of suffering and

---

[4]One memorable but fictional account of Christendom comes from the Netflix production *The Crown*. Queen Mary (grandmother to Elizabeth) describes Christian royalty to the new Queen Elizabeth:

> Monarchy is God's sacred mission to grace and dignify the earth. To give ordinary people an ideal to strive towards, an example of nobility and duty to raise them in their wretched lives. Monarchy is a calling from God. That is why you are crowned in an abbey, not a government building. Why you are anointed, not appointed. It's an archbishop that puts the crown on your head, not a minister or public servant. Which means that you are answerable to God in your duty, not the public. (*The Crown*, "Act of God," directed by Julian Jarrold, written by Peter Morgan, aired November 4, 2016, on Netflix)

glory in such a history—for example, during World War I? What happens when the ruler of the Christian nation is a heretic, or just a really bad Christian? What does it mean for a Christian nation to go to war against a Buddhist or Muslim nation? Does that mean that Jesus is figuratively killing people who do not convert? Under some early Christian rulers, and even for a period of time under the Spanish conquest in the Americas, Christian soldiers did kill the un-repentant indigenes. And what in the world does it mean for Christian nations to engage in slave trading, something the Bible clearly pro-scribes (1 Tim 1:9-11)? And yet with all of these ambiguities, Christi-anity did survive and grow and develop great missionary movements out of Christendom.

It is in missionary work that many ambiguities must be faced. Mis-sionaries often cooperated with, or their work was enhanced by, im-perial nations or multi-national corporations like the British East India Company or the Dutch East India Company. At times, nations that were oppressing local people were helping missionaries open up schools, and they were transporting missionaries to the field. The line between "permission" to serve and "partnering" with a government or company is often a thin and indistinct line. But other ambiguities occur when it comes to methods of recruiting, supporting, and leading people to conversion. Money always creates ambiguities in Christian history. A recent study by Heather D. Curtis highlights these ambiguities regarding financial support to bring about little glo-ries.[5] Her careful study of the *Christian Herald* and its great influence on raising money for the poor raises important questions about the use of power by a very large influential church, a charismatic pastor and editor, and popular religious media. Curtis expresses it well in the introduction. "Like many tales of benevolent campaigns on behalf of 'those less fortunate,' this history exposes how instances of

---

[5]Heather D. Curtis, *Holy Humanitarians: American Evangelicals and Global Aid* (Cambridge, MA: Harvard University Press, 2018).

exceptional generosity have been bound up with personal self-interest and broader political agendas . . . and how the practice of philanthropy has always involved the exercise of privilege, prejudice, and power."[6] Ambiguities like these in Christian history must be faced head on in order to make us sensitive to the ambiguities in our own churches and lives today. Accepting and discussing these historical and present ambiguities keeps us humble and dependent on God, the only wise one.

Read history for our missionary involvement. There is a genre of Christian history called mission history, or history of the missionary movement. Kenneth Scott Latourette wrote such a history focusing on the spread of Christianity as a missionary movement. His *A History of the Expansion of Christianity* set the standard by looking at social and cultural factors that had an influence on the spread of Christianity.[7] He also looked at the "type" of Christianity that was spread and the means by which it spread. His volumes describe Christianity spreading like tides advancing and then receding. Each advancing tide was a little more extensive than the last. His was an optimistic and even progressive approach, an approach that was easily defensible before the second half of the twentieth century. Other Roman Catholic as well as Protestant authors have told mission histories. Our point here is that focusing on the lessons of mission history is another key reason to study Christian history.

Christianity is a missionary faith, what I earlier identified as a religion of cruciform apostolicity. The suffering of the church cannot be separated from the missionary nature of the faith. Christian churches are still called to participate in Jesus' mission in the world, so what does history teach us about our involvement today? It is very important that this history be looked at carefully with all the resources

---

[6] Curtis, *Holy Humanitarians*, 6.
[7] Kenneth Scott Latourette, *A History of the Expansion of Christianity*, 7 vols. (New York: Harper, 1937–1945).

or tools of modern social sciences and even modern critiques regarding gender, empire, culture, and race. As was mentioned above, we will find many ambiguities in studying this history of Christian missionary work.

The spread of Christianity across Russia in the eighteenth and nineteenth centuries is very different from the spread of Christianity in the Pacific Islands. Both were mainly Indigenous or spread from proximate cultures, both were intentional, and both were focused on intentional migration of Christians to spread the teachings of Jesus. And both movements were very effective. However, one was the spread of Orthodox Christianity by monks and priests, and the other was the spread of low church Protestantism by believers who were mostly laypeople.

The missionary work of Augustinians, Franciscans, and later the Jesuits in the Americas has many ambiguities regarding its relationship to the Spanish Conquistadors and Portuguese traders. Luis Rivera called it a violent evangelism.[8] Most of the missionaries accepted views of Indigenous and African people as "infants" in need of parental guidance, at best. Much can be learned for today when we study those who resisted the common assumptions about people who were different. Many of these prophetic missionaries suffered alone, and others actually influenced emperors and empresses by their strong theological and prophetic statements. Early evangelical Protestants working in Africa provide a wealth of examples of both faithfulness and love as well as cultural superiority in their acceptance and at times rejection of African cultural practices.

So many of the divisions and struggles in the contemporary church relate to inculturation or contextualization. The study of missionary policies, theology, and practices must be instructive for us today. This is not just mission history separated from Christian history, but this is seeing the missionary work of the church as an essential dimension

---

[8]Luis N. Rivera, *A Violent Evangelism: The Political and Religious Conquest of the Americas* (Louisville, KY: Westminster John Knox, 1992).

of Christianity in any age. When there is little crosscultural missionary work at all, that also must be instructive for us today.

Read to have a greater awareness of evil. There is so much tragedy
in Christian history. Good people give in to the temptations that
plague all of humankind: passions, avarice, and pride.[9] Sometimes it
is hard to understand how such good people turned so sinful or evil.
And far too often we see churches and Christian organizations that
sell their souls to profit, fame, and influence. It is not just the major
stories that we seek to understand (the German Church under the
Nazis), but it is the subtle and almost imperceptible compromises that
need to be studied and marked for our churches today. How is it that
Christians so blindly follow leaders who are obviously proud and ava-
ricious? And the more important question is how in the world can
leaders who start out with so little and who become great preachers,
bishops, and evangelists be seduced by the trinity of vices?

In the past decades many evangelists have given in to sexual and
materialistic pleasures: buying private jets, owning yachts, day spas,
and multiple homes while they preach "blessed are the poor." And in
recent decades we have report after report of Catholic priests who,
often for years on end, were involved in sexual sins with young boys
and young men. And the church so often looked away or covered up
the systemic sin within the church. The damage to Christian witness
by such failures is hard to measure. Cynics are elated by such revelations, and Christians are put on the defensive. All that can be said is
that it is wrong. The church has failed.

It is important to face these failures understanding that we are observing the persistence of evil. We can talk about psychological conditions or social pressures, but the bottom line for Christians is that evil

---

[9]In the early church these three were often considered the three main vices plaguing the church.
Generally the sin of pride was called "self-esteem," meaning people found their esteem in themselves
rather than in God their Savior. See *The Philokalia*, trans. G. E. H Palmer, Philip Sherrard, and Kallistos Ware, vol. 1 (New York: Faber and Faber, 1979), especially Evagrios the Solitary, "Texts on
Discrimination," 38-52.

is still alive and active, and Christians must respond faithfully as we learn about the persistence of evil in history. We may not have Christian empires forcing their will on people as in the time of Charlemagne or the Conquistadors centuries ago, but we do still have Christians who put their hopes in presidents, judges, and other political leaders, as if such an alliance will be blessed by God. History tells a different story if we will listen carefully and then tell this tragic story well.

The persistence of evil is not just the big and public and widely broadcast occurrences; it is also the unrepentant egos on a church council or among the deacons or vestry. Power, even the little power in a local church, mission agency, Christian college, or seminary, can corrupt others. It is important when reading Christian history to note the places where evil attaches like a leach or barnacle on the church and slowly brings the church down. Divisions, despair, and discouragement seep in when the "self-esteem," passions, or greed of leaders begin to take over the leadership of the church. It is part of Christian history that we should attend to for the sake of healthy congregations today.

Read history to understand the relationship between the kingdom of God and earthly kingdoms. When I was recently teaching Asian Christianity, students were flummoxed by the influence of empires on the rise and fall of Christianity in Asia: Parthian, Sasanian, Abbasid, Tang, and Mongol, among others. Of course this is true all over the world, but it has been especially dramatic in Asia. Often the relationship between the kingdom of God and earthly kingdoms is ambiguous, as when Christian leaders were living in capital cities and had special relationships with kings and emperors. At times like that the church seemed to be compromised. However, the church did have a connection to authorities; it had a voice. At other times emperors welcomed Christian leaders and their churches as a sign of divine blessings on their earthly kingdoms. When emperors like the Mongols welcomed East Syrian bishops as part of the imperial entourage, they were both being used, but they did have a degree of peace.

Christianity is shaped, often reduced, by earthly kingdoms. It is important to study how Christian leaders related to various rulers and their kingdoms, for their responses are instructive today as more and more Western nations are less respectful of Christianity and as the church presses in on non-Christian (even anti-Christian) countries. What can be learned and passed on to Christians in oppressive nations? What can Western Christians learn about suffering and faithfulness when laws and rules turn anti-Christian?

One of the important issues to study is how Christians living under oppressive rulers have remained healthy as a church, evangelizing and discipling their young and developing new and creative ways of being the church in difficult circumstances. This has been evident in many periods in Christian history. In the 1960s and 1970s many Western Christians assumed that Christianity was all but eradicated in China under Mao. It was assumed that the Great Leap Forward and Cultural Revolution had "smoked out" Christians who were then imprisoned, deported to the western regions, or killed. Others denied the faith. I did not know of any Western Christians who were talking about the growth of the church in China under Mao. None. I don't believe Western Christians ever thought there would be stories such as that of Lin Zhao, which has been made available to the English-speaking world in recent years.[10] There are many hundreds of thousands of other untold Chinese Christian stories that are needed to help explain the miracle of Chinese Christianity.

And then there is the story of African Christianity after 1950. It was assumed by well-educated historians that Christianity in Africa was growing because of Christian empires that propped up missionaries and mission agencies. However, the truth was really that African Christianity was being held back by its association with European empires. Only after the independence of nations, and the churches,

---

[10]Lian Xi, *Blood Letters: The Untold Story of Lin Zhao, A Martyr in Mao's China* (New York: Basic Books, 2018).

did Christianity suddenly grow. Western Christian empires held back the growth of African Christianity. This is just another reason why careful historical study is needed.

Read history to learn unity and love. Writing this volume in the early twenty-first century means that certain themes must be lifted up because of the concerns of the present moment and the incarnational nature of Christianity. Christianity must both connect with local cultures and not leave them the same. The gospel is to enter individuals and cultures (through language, customs, habits, and relationships) and, as it were, lift them up and clean them off. *Sanctification* is a good word for the work of God in cultures, but so is *rectification*. Cultures, like individuals, are made in the image of God to represent something of God and his rule in creation.[11] We can expect to see this sanctification expressed in two important themes: unity and love.

Why do I focus on these two themes? I believe Scripture makes it clear that God is concerned to bring about peace, reconciliation, and unity while the forces of evil and Satan himself seek to divide, separate, and kill. Division is seen in the entrance of sin into the world: Adam and Eve begin to blame each other. Cain kills Abel. Even when the nation of Israel is finally formed, it is quickly divided by civil strife (even family strife). The new unity that comes with the teaching and life of Jesus is to create a new community of those who are in Christ. The body of Christ is to show the world how to live together in unity. Church divisions are an anathema to the teachings of Christ and the witness of the church. Jesus' great high priestly prayer is about unity. At the point of suffering and death he is concerned about the mission of his followers who are to be sent into all the world: "As you have sent me into the world, so I have sent them into the world" (Jn 17:18). But his main prayer concern for this mission to be accomplished has to do with unity. Jesus'

---

[11]This concept of cultures being like collective individuals that are meant to represent God is discussed at length in Scott Sunquist, *Understanding Christian Mission: Participation in Suffering and Glory* (Grand Rapids, MI: Baker Academic, 2013), 243-54.

unity with the Father, absolute and essential unity, is to be the same type of unity that Jesus' believers or followers experience: "I ask . . . that they may all be one. As you Father, are in me and I am in you, may they also be in us, so that the world may believe that you have sent me" (Jn 17:20-21). And furthermore, the centrality of this teaching for this volume on history is given throughout John 17. I have emphasized the key themes that come together in this prayer:

> The *glory* that you have given me I have given them, so that they may *be one*, as we *are one*, I in them and you in me, that they may become completely one, so that the world may know that you have sent me and have *loved them* even as you have *loved me*. Father, I desire that those also, whom you have given me, may be with me where I am, to see *my glory*, which you have given me because you *loved me* before the foundation of the world. (Jn 17:22-24)

It is very important that reading the history of Christianity should cause us to ask questions about divisions and to seek to learn greater unity for the future witness of the church.

As this passage also shows us, witness to God's glory in Jesus Christ is related not only to the unity of his disciples but also to love. The love of the Father for the Son is to show through the love seen in the church. "I made your name known to them, and I will make it known, so that the love with which you have loved me may be in them, and I in them" (Jn 17:26). Since God is love, we should look for the revelation of God's love to be evident as a signpost of his glory in history. Christians united in love make God's mission possible and reveal more of his kingdom on earth, as it is in heaven.

Historical study about unity and love for today should focus on instances of the bridging of national, ethnic, racial, and economic divisions. Again, the heavenly vision of all the nations and ethnic groups around the throne is our inspiration; it is the church's hope. Historically there have been times and places where racial barriers have been broken down and the supposed inferiority of certain races has been rejected by the church. Too often we have negative examples where the church too easily accepted a progressivism or paternalism that was based on the inferiority of certain races or ethnicities. Awareness of such anthropological heresies is important as we move forward in God's mission today.

Unfortunately, such ethnocentrism is both very damaging to people's lives, and it is in fact a universal sin found in all cultures and nations. Real families are broken up, and people are denied freedom, jobs, education, and access to the gospel. No one culture owns this sin. We can find examples across the globe and across time. The Christian historian and the Christian reading history of Christianity must look for counterexamples, those people who lived a Christian life of reconciliation, bridge-building, and loving contextualization that brought the kingdom of God to life.

This should be a major concern in the study of Christian history today. There has been enough unmerited suffering caused by racism and ethnocentrism. In addition to telling the stories of Christian failure with honesty, sorrow, and compassion, we must look historically for prophets and pioneers who resisted lower instincts of ethnocentrism based in insecurities and little faith. Hope is the oxygen of the suffering and oppressed. The suffering church continues to move forward with this hope of glory.

A BRIEF POSTSCRIPT ON TEACHING CHRISTIAN HISTORY

Learning is enhanced through curiosity. Historians should begin a history class by finding questions, problems, or cognitive dissonance that will draw students in to ask the important questions and to discover some vital answers. Even this volume started with such a concern: "Western theology is too small for global Christianity today." We want to know what in the world this means!

This volume (or this approach) can be used as a way to draw students into the study of Christian history so that they will learn more and learn how to live. What do I mean by this? Using this book as an introduction begins to raise many questions related to the study that lies ahead. Curiosity is cultivated by suggesting an approach. Concepts such as time (cyclical? progressive?), suffering, sentness, and hope are introduced to open up ways of thinking about the subject. Most books and primary sources that the students will read will not assume these themes. Therefore students will be asking these important questions as they pick up other resources on Christian history.

I think this is most valuable when students read primary sources. Students should be reading many primary sources. Students should have a feel for what people really said in fifth-century Turkey or fifteenth-century Spain and not just take it for granted that the twentieth- or twenty-first-century historian is accurately reporting what happened. The student who has read this book as an "interpreter" or guide for history has an advantage. Each student can ask questions related to this framework. "Does Martin Luther depend upon worldly power for Christian leadership, or is he pushing away from that and embracing a cruciform understanding of leadership? In what way?" And, "What about Martin Luther King Jr.? How do we see his life and teachings expressing the cruciform nature of the Christian life and the hope of glory?" "Can we understand and even critique Christian history in the United States during the 1950s and 1960s through these lenses?"

Of course, I believe this gives our students a great advantage by preparing the mind and even the emotions to study Christian history on its own terms. What we are doing is making it possible for the study of Christian history and also for the study of our contemporary church to be understood and critiqued in meaningful ways. Some will disagree with this approach, but I have offered what my forty years of reading Christian history have led me to believe. I only wish that when I had started studying the history of Christianity I had such guidance or mentoring in what to focus on and how to read. I offer this as your companion along your historical journey into the fascinating and illuminating world of Christian history.

Bibliography

Acolatse, Esther E. *Powers, Principalities, and the Spirit: Biblical Realism in Africa and the West*. Grand Rapids, MI: Eerdmans, 2018.

Allen, Michael. *Grounded in Heaven: Recentering Christian Hope and Life on God*. Grand Rapids, MI: Eerdmans, 2018.

Allison, Dale. *Jesus of Nazareth: Millenarian Prophet*. Minneapolis: Augsburg, 1998.

Anderson, Gerald H., ed. *The Theology of Christian Mission*. New York: McGraw-Hill, 1961.

Baillie, John. *A Diary of Private Prayer*. Edited by Susanna Wright. New York: Scribner, 2014.

Balthasar, Hans Urs von. *A Theology of History*. New York: Sheed and Ward, 1963.

Bantu, Vince. *A Multitude of All Peoples: Engaging Ancient Christianity's Global Identity*. Downers Grove, IL: IVP Academic, 2020.

Barth, Karl. "An Exegetical Study of Matthew 28:16-20." In *The Theology of the Christian Mission*, edited by Gerald Anderson, 55-71. New York: McGraw-Hill, 1961.

Bebbington, D. W. *Patterns in History: A Christian View*. Downers Grove, IL: InterVarsity Press, 1979.

Becker-Cantarino, Barbara, ed. *Migration and Religion: Christian Transatlantic Missions, Islamic Migration to Germany*. Amsterdam: Rodopi, 2012.

Bediako, Kwame. *Christianity in Africa: The Renewal of Non-Western Religion*. Maryknoll, NY: Orbis, 1995.

Behr, John. *Formation of Christian Theology*. Vol. 2, *The Nicene Faith, Part 1*. Crestwood, NY: St. Vladimir's Seminary Press, 2004.

———. *The Mystery of Christ: Life in Death*. Crestwood, NY: St. Vladimir's Seminary Press, 2006.

Bellah, Robert N. *Religion in Human Evolution: From the Paleolithic to the Axial Age*. Cambridge, MA: Belknap, 2011.

Berkhof, Hendrikus. *Christ, the Meaning of History*. Grand Rapids, MI: Baker, 1979.

Bevens, Steven. *Models of Contextual Theology.* Rev. ed. Maryknoll, NY: Orbis, 2002.

Blight, David W. *Frederick Douglass: Prophet of Freedom.* New York: Simon and Schuster, 2018.

Bloch, Marc. *The Historian's Craft.* Delhi, India: Aakar, 2017.

Bradley, James E., and Richard A. Muller, eds. *Church History: An Introduction to Research, Reference Works, and Methods.* Grand Rapids, MI: Eerdmans, 1995.

Bruel, Wolfgang. "Theological Tenets and Motives of Mission: August Hermann Francke, Nikolaus Ludwig von Zinzendorf." In *Migration and Religion: Christian Transatlantic Missions, Islamic Migration to Germany,* edited by Barbara Becker-Cantarino, 41-60. Amsterdam: Rodopi, 2012.

Bultmann, Rudolf. *History and Eschatology: The Presence of Eternity.* New York: Harper and Row, 1962.

Bühlmann, Walbert. *The Coming of the Third Church: An Analysis of the Present and Future of the Church.* Maryknoll, NY: Orbis, 1977.

Butterfield, Herbert. *The Origins of History.* New York: Basic Books, 1981.

Cairns, Earle E. *God and Man in Time: A Christian Approach to Historiography.* Grand Rapids, MI: Baker, 1979.

Césaire, Aimé. *Discourse on Colonialism (Discours sur le colonialism).* New York: Monthly Review, 2000.

Charney, Israel W., ed. *The Encyclopedia of Genocide.* 2 vols. Santa Barbara: ABC-CLIO, 1999.

Cheng, Eileen Ka-May. *Historiography: An Introductory Guide.* New York: Continuum, 2012.

Chow, Alexander, and Emma Wild-Wood, eds. *Studies in World Christianity: The Edinburgh Review of Theology and Religion* 22, no. 3 (2016).

Clark, Elizabeth A. *Founding the Fathers: Early Church History and Protestant Professors in Nineteenth-Century America.* Philadelphia: University of Pennsylvania Press, 2011.

Collingwood, R. G. *The Idea of History.* Rev. ed. New York: Oxford University Press, 1994.

Curtis, Heather D. *Holy Humanitarians: American Evangelicals and Global Aid.* Cambridge, MA: Harvard University Press, 2018.

D'Arcy, M. C., SJ. *The Sense of History: Secular and Sacred.* London: Faber and Faber, 1959.

Dayfoot, Arthur Charles. *The Shaping of the West Indian Church, 1492–1962.* Gainesville: University Press of Florida, 1998.

Dennis, James S. *Christian Missions and Social Progress: A Sociological Study of Foreign Missions.* 3 vols. New York: Fleming H. Revell, 1897–1906.

———. *Foreign Missions After a Century.* New York: Fleming H. Revell, 1893.

Eddy, Mary Baker. *Science and Health with Key to the Scriptures.* Boston: Christian Science Publishing Society, 1917.

Ehrman, Bart D. *Lost Christianities: The Battles for Scripture and the Faiths We Never Knew.* New York: Oxford University Press, 2003.

―――. *Lost Scriptures: Books That Did Not Make It into the New Testament*. New York: Oxford University Press, 2003.

―――. *Misquoting Jesus: The Story Behind Who Changed the Bible and Why*. New York: HarperSanFrancisco, 2005.

Fairbairn, Donald. *Life in the Trinity: An Introduction to Theology with the Help of the Church Fathers*. Downers Grove, IL: IVP Academic, 2009.

Fisher, Daniel W. *Calvin Wilson Mateer: Forty-Five Years as a Missionary in Shantung, China; A Biography*. Philadelphia: Westminster, 1911.

Florovsky, Georges. "The Predicament of the Christian Historian." In *God, History and the Historians: An Anthology of Modern Christian History*, edited by C. T. McIntire, 406-42. New York: Oxford University Press, 1977.

Foucault, Michel. *The Order of Things: An Archaeology of the Human Sciences*. London: Routledge, 1970.

Gay, Peter. *Style in History: Gibbon, Ranke, Macaulay, Burckhardt*. New York: W. W. Norton, 1974.

Grandberg-Michaelson, Wesley. *From Times Square to Timbuktu: The Post-Christian West Meets the Non-Western Church*. Grand Rapids, MI: Eerdmans, 2013.

Green, Anna, and Kathleen Troup, eds. *The Houses of History: A Critical Reader in Twentieth-Century History and Theory*. New York: New York University Press, 1999.

Green, Jay D. *Christian Historiography: Five Rival Versions*. Waco, TX: Baylor University Press, 2015.

Greenblatt, Stephen. *Marvelous Possessions: The Wonder of the New World*. Chicago: University of Chicago Press, 1991.

Grenz, Stanley J. *A Primer on Postmodernism*. Grand Rapids, MI: Eerdmans, 1996.

Hanciles, Jehu J. *Beyond Christendom: Globalization, African Migration, and the Transformation of the West*. Maryknoll, NY: Orbis, 2008.

Headley, John M. *Church, Empire and World: The Quest for Universal Order, 1520–1640*. Brookfield, VT: Ashgate, 1997.

Hiebert, Paul G. "Conversion, Cultures, and Cognitive Categories." *Gospel in Context* 1, no. 4 (1978): 24-29.

Himmelfarb, Gertrude. *The New History and the Old: Critical Essays and Reappraisals*. Rev. ed. Cambridge, MA: Harvard University Press, 2004.

Iggers, Georg G., *Historiography in the Twentieth Century: From Scientific Objectivity to the Postmodern Challenge*. Middletown, CT: Wesleyan University Press, 2005.

Irvin, Dale T. *Christian Histories, Christian Traditioning: Rendering Accounts*. Maryknoll, NY: Orbis, 1998.

Irvin, Dale T., and Scott W. Sunquist. *History of the World Christian Movement*. 2 vols. Maryknoll, NY: Orbis, 2001–2012.

Isichei, Elizabeth. *A History of Christianity in Africa: From Antiquity to the Present*. Grand Rapids, MI: Eerdmans, 1995.

Jaki, Stanley L. "Genesis 1: A Cosmogenesis?" *Homiletic and Pastoral Review* 94, no. 3 (1993): 28-32, 61-64.

Jenkins, Philip. *The Next Christendom: The Coming of Global Christianity.* Oxford: Oxford University Press, 2002.

Kalu, Ogbu U. *Clio in a Sacred Garb: Essays on Christian Presence and African Responses, 1900–2000.* Trenton, NJ: Africa World Press, 2008.

———. *The Collected Essays of Ogbu Uke Kalu.* Vol. 2, *Christian Missions in Africa: Success, Ferment and Trauma.* Edited by Wilhelmina J. Kalu, Nimi Wariboko, and Toyin Falola. Trenton, NJ: Africa World Press, 2010.

Kalu, Ogbu U., and Aaline Low, eds. "Changing Tides: Some Currents in World Christianity at the Opening of the Twenty-First Century." In *Interpreting Contemporary Christianity: Global Processes and Local Identities,* 3-23. Grand Rapids, MI: Eerdmans, 2008.

Keazor, Ed Emeka. "Igbo Historiography: Milestones, Triumphs and Challenges." Paper delivered at the Igbo Conference, School of Oriental and African Studies, London, April 21, 2018.

King, Karen L. *What Is Gnosticism?* Cambridge, MA: Harvard University Press, 2003.

Kipling, Rudyard. "White Man's Burden: The United States and the Philippine Islands." *McClure's Magazine,* February 1899.

Kolodiejchuk, Brian, ed. *Mother Teresa: Come Be My Light: The Private Writings of the Saint of Calcutta.* New York: Doubleday, 2007.

Korschorke, Klaus, ed. *African Identites and World Christianity in the Twentieth Century: Proceedings of the Third International Munich-Freising Conference on the History of Christianity in the Non-Western World, September 15–17, 2004.* Wiesbaden: Otto Harrassowitz, 2005.

Kreider, Alan. *The Patient Ferment of the Early Church: The Improbable Rise of Christianity in the Roman Empire.* Grand Rapids, MI: Baker Academic, 2016.

Latourette, Kenneth Scott. *A History of Christianity.* Vol. 1, *Beginnings to 1500.* Rev. ed. New York: Harper and Row, 1975.

———. *A History of the Expansion of Christianity.* 7 vols. New York: Harper and Brothers, 1937–1945.

Leibrecht, Walter, ed. *Religion and Culture: Essays in Honor of Paul Tillich.* New York: Harper and Row, 1959.

Lewis, Donald M. *The Origins of Christian Zionism: Lord Shaftesbury and Evangelical Support for a Jewish Homeland.* Cambridge: Cambridge University Press, 2010.

Louth, Andrew, ed. and trans. *Maximus the Confessor.* London: Routledge, 1996.

———. *The Origins of the Christian Mystical Tradition: From Plato to Denys.* 2nd ed. Oxford: Oxford University Press, 2007.

Mackay, John A. *Ecumenics: The Science of the Church Universal.* Englewood Cliffs, NJ: Prentice-Hall, 1964.

May, Gerhard. *Creatio Ex Nihilo: The Doctrine of "Creation Out of Nothing" in Early Christian Thought.* Translated by A. S. Worrall. Edinburgh: T&T Clark, 1994.

MacMullen, Ramsay. *Christianizing the Roman Empire, AD 100–400.* New Haven: Yale University Press, 1984.

Mateer, Robert M. *Character-Building in China: The Life-Story of Julia Brown Mateer.* New York: Fleming H. Revell, 1912.

Mbiti, John S. *African Religions and Philosophy.* London: Heinemann, 1969.

McAlister, Malani. *The Kingdom of God Has No Borders: A Global History of American Evangelicals.* New York: Oxford University Press, 2018.

McIlwain, C. H., A. Myendorf, and J. L. Morrison. "Bias in Historical Writing." *History* 11, no. 43 (1926): 193-203.

McIntire, C. T. *God, History, and Historians: An Anthology of Modern Christian Views of History.* New York: Oxford University Press, 1977.

McNeill, William H., and Mitsuko Iriye, eds. *Readings in World History.* Vol. 9, *Modern Asia and Africa.* New York: Oxford University Press, 1971.

Mandryk, Jason. *Operation World.* Downers Grove, IL: InterVarsity Press, 2021.

Mead, Sidney E. *History and Identity.* Missoula, MT: Scholars Press, 1979.

Mignolo, Walter D. *Local Histories/Global Designs: Coloniality, Subaltern Knowledges, and Border Thinking.* Princeton: Princeton University Press, 2000.

Moltmann, Jürgen. *The Experiment Hope.* Edited and translated by M. Douglas Meeks. Philadelphia: Fortress, 1975.

———. *The Future of Hope: Theology as Eschatology.* New York: Herder and Herder, 1970.

Morgan, Peter. *The Crown.* Netflix, 2016.

Mosheim, Johann Lorenz von. *Institutes of Ecclesiastical History, Ancient and Modern.* Edited by H. Soames. Translated by J. Murdock. London: Longman, 1841.

Murphey, Murray G. *Truth and History.* Albany, NY: SUNY Press, 2009.

Nash, Ronald H. *Christian Faith and Historical Understanding.* Grand Rapids, MI: Zondervan, 1984.

Newbigin, Lesslie. *The Gospel in a Pluralist Society.* Grand Rapids, MI: Eerdmans, 1989.

———. *The Household of God: Lectures on the Nature of the Church.* London: SCM Press, 1957.

———. *A Walk Through the Bible.* London: SPCK, 1999.

O'Donovan, Oliver. *The Ways of Judgment.* Grand Rapids, MI: Eerdmans, 2005.

O'Mahony, Anthony, ed. *Christianity in the Middle East: Studies in Modern History, Theology, and Politics.* London: Melisende, 2008.

Pelikan, Jaroslav. "The Predicament of the Christian Historian: A Case Study." *Reflections: Center of Theological Inquiry* 1 (1998): 26-47.

Pelta, Kathy. *Discovering Christopher Columbus: How History Is Invented.* Minneapolis: Lerner, 1991.

Peterson, Jordan B. *12 Rules for Life: An Antidote to Chaos.* Toronto: Random House, 2018.

Phan, Peter. *Asian Christianities: History, Theology, Practice.* Maryknoll, NY: Orbis, 2018.

———. *Mission and Catechesis: Alexandre de Rhodes and Inculturation in Seventeenth Century Vietnam.* Maryknoll, NY: Orbis, 2006.

Philokalia. Translated by G. E. H. Palmer, Philip Sherrard, and Kallistos Ware. 4 vols. New York: Faber and Faber, 1979.

Ramachandra, Vinoth. *The Recovery of Mission: Beyond the Pluralist Paradigm.* Grand Rapids, MI: Eerdmans, 1996.

Rauschenbusch, Walter. *A Theology for the Social Gospel.* Nashville: Abingdon, 1917.

Resnick, Brian. "Intellectual Humility: The Importance of Knowing You Might Be Wrong." Vox.com. January 4, 2019. www.vox.com/science-and-health/2019/1/4/17989224/intellectual-humility-explained-psychology-replication.

Richardson, Cyril C., ed. and trans. *Early Christian Fathers.* New York: Macmillan, 1970.

Richardson, Don. *Eternity in Their Hearts.* Ventura, CA: Regal, 1981.

Rivera, Luis N. *A Violent Evangelism: The Political and Religious Conquest of the Americas.* Louisville, KY: Westminster John Knox, 1994.

Rogich, Daniel M. *Serbian Patericon: Saints of the Serbian Orthodox Church.* Vol 1. Platina, CA: Saint Herman, 1994.

Rogonzinski, Jan. *A Brief History of the Caribbean: From the Arawak and Carib to the Present.* Rev. ed. New York: Plume, 2000.

Rose, Fr. Seraphim. *Genesis, Creation, and Early Man: The Orthodox Christian Vision.* Platina, CA: St. Herman, 2000.

Sale, Kirkpatrick. *The Conquest of Paradise: Christopher Columbus and the Columbian Legacy.* New York: Plume, 1991.

Sanneh, Lamin, *Disciples of all Nations: Pillars of World Christianity.* Oxford: Oxford University Press. 2008.

———. *Encountering the West: Christianity and the Global Cultural Process.* Maryknoll, NY: Orbis, 1993.

———. *Translating the Message: The Missionary Impact on Culture.* Maryknoll, NY: Orbis, 1989.

———. *Whose Religion Is Christianity? The Gospel Beyond the West.* Grand Rapids, MI: Eerdmans, 2003.

Sanneh, Lamin, and Joel A. Carpenter, eds. *The Changing Face of Christianity: Africa, the West, and the World.* Oxford: Oxford University Press, 2005.

Sayers, Dorothy. *Creed or Chaos: Why Christians Must Choose Either Dogma or Disaster, or Why It Really Does Matter What You Believe.* London: Hodder and Stoughton, 1939.

Schaff, Philip, ed. *The Nicene and Post-Nicene Fathers, First Series.* Vol. 9. Peabody, MA: Hendrickson, 2004.

Schnitker, Sarah. "An Examination of Patience and Well-Being." *Journal of Positive Psychology* 7, no. 4 (2012): 263-80.

Sharkey, Heather. "An Egyptian in China: Ahmed Fahmy and the Making of World Christianities." *Church History* 78, no. 2 (2009): 309-26.

Shaw, Mark, and Wanjiru M. Gitau. *The Kingdom of God in Africa: A History of African Christianity*. Rev. ed. Carlisle, UK: Langham Global Library, 2020.

Shenk, Wilbert R. ed. *Enlarging the Story: Perspectives on Writing World Christian History*. Maryknoll, NY: Orbis, 2002.

Sider, J. Alexander. *To See History Doxologically: History and Holiness in John Howard Yoder's Ecclesiology*. Grand Rapids, MI: Eerdmans, 2011.

Simpler, Steven H. *Roland H. Bainton: An Examination of His Reformation Historiography*. Lewiston, NY: Edwin Mellen, 1985.

Speer, Robert E. *The Finality of Jesus Christ*. New York: Fleming H. Revell, 1933.

Spence, Jonathan D. *God's Chinese Son: The Taiping Heavenly Kingdom of Hong Xiuquan*. New York: W.W. Norton, 1996.

Stannard, David E. *American Holocaust: Columbus and the Conquest of the New World*. New York: Oxford University Press, 1992.

Sterk, Andrea, and Nina Caputo. *Faithful Narratives: Historians, Religion, and the Challenge of Objectivity*. Ithaca, NY: Cornell University Press, 2014.

Strahan, James. *Hebrew Ideals: A Study of Genesis 11–50*. 4th ed. Edinburgh: T&T Clark, 1922.

Sunquist, Scott W. *Explorations in Asian Christianity: History, Theology, and Mission*. Downers Grove, IL: IVP Academic, 2017.

———. "Hidden History." *Christian Century*, September 18, 2006. https://www.christian century.org/reviews/2006-09/hidden-history.

———. "Julia Brown Mateer." Paper presented to World Mission Celebration Conference of PC(USA), Cincinnati, October 23, 2009.

———. "Missio Dei: Christian History Envisioned as Cruciform Apostolicity." *Missiology* 37, no. 1 (2009): 33-46.

———. "Narsai and the Persians." PhD diss., Princeton Theological Seminary, 1990.

———. "Time, the Lectures, and Redemption." *Princeton Seminary Bulletin* 30 (2009): 180-92.

———. *Understanding Christian Mission: Participation in Suffering and Glory*. Grand Rapids, MI: Baker Academic, 2013.

———. *The Unexpected Christian Century: The Reversal and Transformation of Global Christianity, 1900–2000*. Grand Rapids, MI: Baker Academic, 2015.

Sunquist, Scott W., David Wu Chu Sing, and John Chew Hiang Chea, eds. *A Dictionary of Asian Christianity*. Grand Rapids, MI: Eerdmans, 2001.

Swanstrom, Roy. *History in the Making: An Introduction to the Study of the Past*. Downers Grove, IL: InterVarsity Press, 1978.

Tillich, Paul. "Missions in World History." In *The Theology of the Christian Mission*, edited by Gerald H. Anderson, 281-89. New York: McGraw-Hill, 1961.

Tisby, Jemar. *The Color of Compromise: The Truth About the American Church's Complicity in Racism*. Grand Rapids, MI: Zondervan, 2019.

Todorov, Tzvetan. *The Conquest of America: The Question of the Other*. Translated by Richard Howard. New York: Harper and Row, 1984.

Trimbur, Dominique. "Between Eastern and Western Christendom: The Benedictines, France and the Syrian Catholic Church in Jerusalem." In *Christianity in the Middle East, Studies in Modern History, Theology, and Politics*, edited by Anthony O' Mahony 375-421. London: Melisende, 2008.

Van Dusen, Henry P. *World Christianity: Yesterday, Today, Tomorrow*. New York: Abingdon, 1942.

Vischer, Lukas, ed. *Church History in an Ecumenical Perspective: Papers and Reports of an International Ecumenical Consultation Held in Basel, October 12–17, 1981*. Bern: Evangelische Arbeitsstelle Oekumene Schweiz, 1982.

———. *Towards a History of the Church in the Third World: The Issue of Periodisation*. Bern: Evangelische Arbeitsstelle Oekumene Schweiz, 1985.

Walls, Andrew F. *The Cross-Cultural Process in Christian History: Studies in the Transmission and Appropriation of Faith*. Maryknoll, NY: Orbis, 2002.

———. "The Mission of the Church Today in the Light of Global History." *Word and World* 20, no. 1 (Winter 2000): 17-21.

Wei, Francis C. M. *The Spirit of Chinese Culture*. New York: Charles Scribner's Sons, 1947.

Wells, Ronald A., ed. *History and the Christian Historian*. Grand Rapids, MI: Eerdmans, 1988.

Wengert, Timothy J., and Charles W. Brockwell Jr., eds. *Telling the Churches' Stories: Ecumenical Perspectives on Writing Christian History*. Grand Rapids, MI: Eerdmans, 1995.

Williams, Patrick, and Laura Chrisman, eds. *Colonial Discourse and Post-Colonial Theory: A Reader*. New York: Columbia University Press, 1994.

Windschuttle, Keith. *The Killing of History: How Literary Critics and Social Theorists Are Murdering Our Past*. San Francisco, CA: Encounter, 1996.

Woodberry, Robert. "The Missionary Roots of Liberal Democracy." *The American Political Science Review* 106, no. 2 (2012): 244-74.

World Christianities Overview. University of Cambridge Faculty of Divinity. www.divinity.cam.ac.uk/researchareas/research-areas/wc#section-3.

Xi, Lian. *Blood Letters: The Untold Story of Lin Zhao: A Martyr in Mao's China*. New York: Basic Books, 2018.

Zurlo, Gina A., and Todd M. Johnson, eds. *World Christian Encyclopedia*. 3rd ed. Edinburgh: Edinburgh University Press, 2019.

General Index

Scripture Index